Invitation to Languages

Foreign Language Exploratory Program

Conrad J. Schmitt

Workbook
and
Audio Activities Booklet

Mc Graw Hill **Glencoe**

New York, New York   Columbus, Ohio   Chicago, Illinois   Peoria, Illinois   Woodland Hills, California

Send all inquiries to:
Glencoe/McGraw-Hill
8787 Orion Place
Columbus, OH 43240-4027

ISBN 0-07-860580-6

Printed in the United States of America.

8 9 10 HSO 10 09

Table of Contents

Welcome to *Spanish!*

Saludos

A Select an appropriate response and circle the corresponding letter.

1. ¡Hola!
   a. ¡Hola!
   b. Gracias.
   c. Estupendo.

2. ¿Qué tal?
   a. Gracias.
   b. ¿Y tú?
   c. Muy bien.

3. Buenos días.
   a. Buenas noches.
   b. Estupendo.
   c. Buenos días.

B In the illustrations below, which people are probably saying *hola* and which are probably saying *buenos días?* Write A for those saying *hola* and B for those saying *buenos días.*

1. _____

2. _____

3. _____

4. _____

5. _____

Invitation to Languages

C **Look at these clocks. Match each clock with the appropriate expression.**

1. Buenas noches. _____   **2.** Buenas tardes. _____   **3.** Buenos días. _____

a.   b.   c.

A.M.   P.M.   P.M.

D **Just as English speakers use abbreviations, Spanish speakers also abbreviate words. Here are a few examples:**

Señor — Sr.
Señora — Sra.
Señorita — Srta.

Note that the abbreviation "Ms." does not exist in Spanish.

Address envelopes to the following people in Spanish using abbreviations.

1. Miss Alicia Salas   _____

2. Mr. Juan Ayerbe   _____

3. Mrs. Cecilia Guzmán _____

2 A*diós*

A Decide who's saying what. Write the appropriate letter next to the illustration.

    a. ¡Hola!   **b.** Adiós.   **c.** Chao.

1. ____

2. ____

3. ____

B Tell if the following farewells are formal (F) or informal (I).

1. Adiós, señor. ____   **2.** Hasta luego, Paco. ____

3. Chao. ____   **4.** Hasta mañana, señora Morales. ____

C Say these Spanish words carefully.

hola   hasta

There is one letter that you did not hear. It is not pronounced in Spanish.

What letter is it? ____

Now say the following Spanish words.

hotel   hospital

3 En clase

A **Match the word with the picture.**

a. una mesa   b. una silla   c. una mochila
d. una calculadora e. un lápiz   f. un bolígrafo
g. un cuaderno   h. una goma

1. ____

2. ____

3. ____

4. ____

5. ____

6. ____

7. ____

8. ____

B **Match the things that you usually use together.**

A   B

1. una mesa y _____   **a.** un bolígrafo

2. un lápiz y _____   **b.** un borrador

3. una tiza y _____   **c.** una goma

4. una hoja de papel y _____   **d.** una silla

C **Circle the letter of the best follow-up to *por favor*.**

1. Por favor.
   a. ¡Hola!
   b. Gracias.
   c. Chao.

D **Write the missing letter of each word.**

g____ma

t____za

bo____ígrafo

computado____a

____loc

Now put the missing letters together to form a word. _____

4 Números

A Write the number.

1. ocho _____

2. dieciocho _____

3. veintiocho _____

4. ochenta y ocho _____

5. ochocientos _____

6. ocho mil _____

B Write the number.

1. siete _____

2. setenta _____

3. setecientos _____

4. nueve _____

5. noventa _____

6. novecientos _____

7. cinco _____

8. quince _____

9. quinientos _____

C Write down the following telephone numbers.

1. tres, cuarenta y cinco, setenta, ochenta y nueve

   _____

2. cinco, treinta y tres, cuarenta y ocho, cincuenta

   _____

D Write the following famous years in American and Spanish history.

  1. mil setecientos setenta y seis _____

  2. mil cuatrocientos noventa y dos _____

  3. mil novecientos treinta y seis _____

Use the years in Activity D to tell when these events happened.

  1. el descubrimiento de América _____

  2. la independencia de los Estados Unidos de América _____

  3. la guerra civil española _____

E Connect the dots.

¿Qué animal es?

a. un tigre

b. un elefante

c. un león

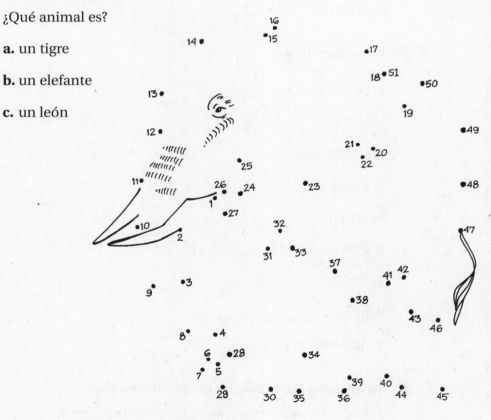

F **Write the letter of the name of the money.**

a. euro   **b.** quetzal
c. peso

1. ____

2. ____

3. ____

WELCOME TO SPANISH

5 *La cortesía*

A **Circle the letter of the best response.**

1. ¡Hola!
   a. Adiós.
   b. ¡Hola! ¿Qué tal?
   c. De nada.

2. Gracias, señor.
   a. No hay de qué.
   b. Sí.
   c. Chao.

B **Circle the letter of the best follow-up.**

1. Una hoja de papel, por favor.
   a. De nada.
   b. ¡Hola!
   c. Gracias.

C **Circle the letter of the expression that doesn't fit.**

1. ¡Hola!
   a. Chao.
   b. Buenos días.
   c. Gracias.

2. Hasta luego.
   a. ¿Qué tal?
   b. Hasta pronto.
   c. Buenas noches.

3. Muy bien.
   a. Estupendo.
   b. Bien, gracias.
   c. ¿Y tú?

D **Look at this menu in a Mexican restaurant. Work with a classmate. Each of you will tell what you are going to order. If you aren't sure what something is, find out from someone in the class. For example, you can ask:** *¿Qué es un burrito?*

Café Tacuba

Ensalada de tomate	100 pesos
Guacamole	100 pesos
Sopa de tortilla	50 pesos
Taco	250 pesos
Enchilada	275 pesos
Burrito	240 pesos
Tostada	200 pesos

E Look at these pictures. Notice that each dish is called a *tortilla*. A *tortilla* in Mexico is a type of pancake made from either corn meal or flour. A *tortilla* in Spain is an egg omelette. A typical Spanish *tortilla* is called *una tortilla a la española.* It is an egg omelette made with potatoes and onions.

una tortilla

una tortilla a la española

La cortesía

⑥ L*a hora*

A **Match the time with each clock.**

a. Es la una.   **b.** Son las dos y media.
c. Son las tres y veinte.   **d.** Son las diez y cuarto.
e. Son las once treinta y cinco. **f.** Son las ocho menos veinte.

1. ____   **2.** ____   **3.** ____

4. ____   **5.** ____   **6.** ____

B **Match the expressions that mean the same thing.**

1. ____ Son las tres y media.   **a.** Son las tres (y) quince.

2. ____ Son las tres y cuarto.   **b.** Son las dos cuarenta y cinco.

3. ____ Son las tres menos cuarto. **c.** Son las tres (y) treinta.

C **Fill out your class schedule in Spanish. Some subjects you may want to use are:**

matemáticas
inglés
español (lenguas)
historia (ciencias sociales)
ciencia (biología, física)
computadora (informática)
educación física
música
arte

Hora	Clase

Los *colores*

A What colors would you need to color the sky, the clouds, and the grass in a picture of a park on a beautiful spring day? Answer in Spanish.

_____

B Color this bird in at least three colors and label them in Spanish.

_____

C Design a flag for your school and color it. Label the colors in Spanish.

_____

⑧ Los días de la semana

A **Each of the following words has a missing letter. Write the missing letter.**

vier____es

____unes

j____eves

miércole____

mart____s

Now unscramble the missing letters to spell a day of the week in Spanish.

_____

B **In English, the days of the week are written with a capital letter. In Spanish, they are written with a small letter:** *lunes, martes, miércoles, jueves, viernes, sábado, domingo.* **Write a capital "A" next to the expression that means "capital letter" and a small "a" next to the expression that means "small letter."**

una letra mayúscula   ____

una letra minúscula   ____

C **Read the following.**

En una semana hay siete días. Los siete días de la semana son: lunes, martes, miércoles, jueves, viernes, sábado y domingo.

In Spanish, the expression *ocho días* **refers to a week.** *Quince días* **refers to two weeks. If there are seven days in a week, can you guess why Spanish speakers refer to the week as eight days and two weeks as fifteen days?**

_____

_____

_____

_____

9 Los meses y las estaciones

A **Complete the answers to the following questions.**

1. ¿Cuántos meses hay en un año?

   Hay _____ meses en un año.

2. ¿Cuántos días hay en una semana?

   Hay _____ días en una semana.

3. ¿Cuántas estaciones hay en un año?

   Hay _____ estaciones en un año.

B **Choose the correct months.**

1. los meses del invierno   ____   **a.** junio, julio y agosto

2. los meses de la primavera ____   **b.** marzo, abril y mayo

3. los meses del verano   ____   **c.** diciembre, enero y febrero

4. los meses del otoño   ____   **d.** septiembre, octubre y noviembre

C **Complete with true information.**

Mi cumpleaños es en el mes de _____. La fecha de mi

cumpleaños es el ____ de _____.

D **Answer the following questions.**

1. ¿Cuál es la fecha de hoy? _____

2. ¿Qué día es mañana? _____

E **Write the months and seasons when people usually do these activities.**

1. el fútbol _____

2. el béisbol _____

3. el esquí _____

10 El tiempo

A Write the letter of the sentence next to the picture that goes with it.

a. Está nevando.   **b.** Hace mucho frío.   **c.** Hace calor.
d. Hay sol.   **e.** Hace viento.

1. _____

2. _____

3. _____

5. _____

4. _____

B Circle the letters of the expressions that can be used to support the numbered sentences. There may be more than one answer.

1. Hace buen tiempo.
    a. Está lloviendo.
    b. Hay sol.
    c. Hace calor.
    d. Está nevando.
    e. El sol brilla.

2. Hace mal tiempo.
    a. Está lloviendo.
    b. Está nevando.
    c. Hay sol.
    d. Hace mucho frío.
    e. Hace un tiempo estupendo.

11 Yo soy...

A **Write *sí* after each true sentence and *no* after each false one.**

1. When Spanish speakers talk about themselves, they say *yo*. ____

2. When Spanish speakers speak to a friend, they say *tú* . ____

3. Spanish speakers use the same verb form with *yo* and *tú*. ____

B **Complete the following conversations with *soy* or *eres*.**

1. ¡Hola! ¿Quién _____?

¿Yo? Yo _____ José. José Garza.

2. ¡Hola! ¿Tú _____ Anita?

Sí, _____ Anita Torres.

Y tú, ¿quién _____?

C **After you complete the conversations in Activity B, get together with a classmate. Perform the conversations together.**

12 Soy de...

A Look at this map. Then circle the letter of the response that gives true information about you.

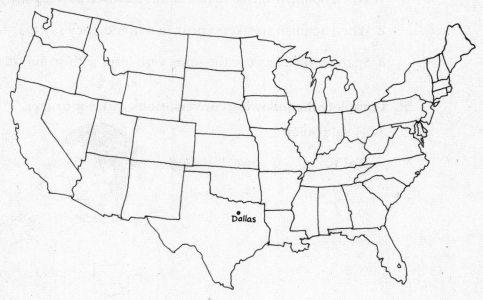

1. ¿Eres de los Estados Unidos?
  a. Sí, soy de los Estados Unidos.
  b. No, no soy de los Estados Unidos.

2. ¿Eres de Dallas?
  a. Sí, soy de Dallas.
  b. No, no soy de Dallas.

If you answered no to either of the above questions, complete these sentences with true information.

1. Yo no soy de los Estados Unidos. Soy de _____.

2. No soy de Dallas. Soy de _____.

B Underline the correct question word.

1. ¿(Quién, Qué) es?
  Es Anita Salas.

2. ¿(Quién, Qué) es?
  Es una calculadora.

3. Soy Diego Martínez.
  Perdón, ¿(quién, qué) eres?

4. Es Susana Dávila.
  Perdón, ¿(quién, qué) es?

5. Es una mochila.
  Perdón, ¿(quién, qué) es?

C **Answer the following questions about yourself. Girls will answer 1 to 3 and boys will answer 4 to 6.**

1. ¿Quién eres?

_____

2. ¿Eres americana o mexicana?

_____

3. ¿De dónde eres?

_____

4. ¿Quién eres?

_____

5. ¿Eres americano o mexicano?

_____

6. ¿De dónde eres?

_____

D **Complete these sentences with the letter -o or -a.**

1. José es mexican____.

2. José no es american____.

3. Y Debbi es american____.

4. Debbi no es mexican____.

5. Yo soy _____.

Debbi

José

Soy de...

E **Complete the story using either *es, soy* or *eres*.**

David _____ americano. David no _____ mexicano. Pepe _____

mexicano. ¿Y tú? ¿Qué _____ ? ¿ _____ de los Estados Unidos?

Yo _____ de _____ (name of city or town).

F **Choose the correct question word.**

Qué   Quién   De dónde

1. ¿ _____ es?   **2.** ¡Hola! ¿ _____ eres?

3. ¿ _____ es Elena?

13 Hablo español

A Look at this map. Spanish is the language spoken in each of these countries. Can you name any of the capitals of these countries?

_____

_____

_____

_____

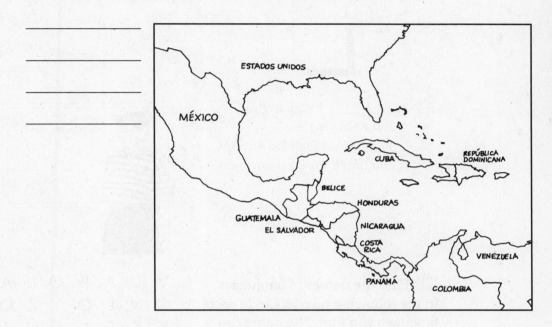

B Complete the answers to the following questions. Then work with a classmate. Ask and answer the questions together.

1. —¿Tú habl____ ruso?

   —No, yo no habl____ ruso.

   —¿No?

   —Yo, no. Pero Igor habl____ ruso.

2. —¿Habl____ inglés?

   —¿Quién? ¿Yo?

   —Sí, tú.

   —Sí, habl____ inglés. Habl____ inglés y español.

C Complete the sentences with question words that make sense.

1. ¿ _____ habla español?
Ramona habla español.
Ella es de la Argentina.

2. Y, ¿ _____ habla Antonio?
Antonio habla italiano.
Él es de Italia.

3. ¿ _____ habla inglés?
Bill habla inglés.
Él es de los Estados Unidos.
Bill habla español también.

D Find the names of languages in the following puzzle. Circle each language you find. The name can be read from left to right, right to left, top to bottom, bottom to top, or diagonally.

Word Bank

árabe	chino
español	francés
inglés	japonés
latín	polaco
ruso	

```
V L A P O L A C O
O X L O Y Z Q H S
Y S É L G N I I U
J O T A L I M N R
A A E C E Á N O O
P M P O S R R I P
B E L O Ñ A P S E
L A T I N B C L R
F R A N C É S G T
O L L O E L S E E
```

When you have completed the puzzle, use the letters printed in boldface to form a word. The letters spell the name of a person.

___ ___ ___ ___ ___

Then change one letter in the name to make a new word.

___ ___ ___ ___ ___

14 Estudio...

A Match the subject with the book cover.

a. latín   b. historia   c. biología
d. música   e. geometría   f. arte

1. ____

2. ____

3. ____

4. ____

5. ____

6. ____

B Complete each of the following words with the missing letters.

1. la esc ____ ____ la

2. yo estud ____ ____

3. la leng ____ ____

4. la c ____ ____ nc ____ ____

5. la histor ____ ____

C Look at the school schedule you wrote in Lesson 6 page 12 of the Workbook. Use it to complete this paragraph.

Yo estudio _____. La clase de _____ es a _____.

El profesor (La profesora) de _____ es el señor (la señora, la señorita)

_____.

D Some classes are easy *(fácil)* and others are difficult *(difícil)*. Look at your schedule and rate all of your classes.

La clase de _____ es fácil.　　　La clase de _____ es fácil.

La clase de _____ es difícil.　　La clase de _____ es difícil.

E Complete the following conversation with the missing letters *-as* or *-o*.

—María, ¿estudi____ español?

—Sí, estudi____ español.

—¿Dónde estudi____ español?

—Pues, estudi____ español en la escuela.

—¿Es interesante la clase de español?

—Sí, es muy interesante. Y no es muy difícil.

—¿Tú habl____ mucho en la clase de español?

—Sí, mucho. Pero no habl____ inglés. Habl____ solamente en español.

F Now complete the following story about María by filling in the missing letters.

María estudi____ español. Estudi____ español en la escuela. La clase de

español es muy interesante. María habl____ mucho en la clase. Pero no

habl____ inglés. Sólo habl____ español.

15 M*i casa*

A **Label the rooms of this house.**

1. la sala   **2.** el comedor   **3.** la cocina
4. el cuarto de dormir   **5.** el cuarto de baño

B **Spanish is spoken in many countries. You will sometimes hear a different word used for the same thing depending upon where you are in the Spanish-speaking world. The word for "bedroom" is an example. If you use the term *cuarto de dormir,* everyone will understand you. But there are some other ways to say bedroom. They are:**

el cuarto
la recámara
la habitación
el dormitorio

C **Look at this house and write** *sí* **after each true sentence and** *no*
after each false one.

   1. Hay un carro en el garaje.   ____

   2. Hay muchas rosas en el jardín.   ____

   3. Hay veinte cuartos en la casa.   ____

   4. Hay un jardín alrededor de la casa. ____

D **There are many Spanish words that are used in English. Read the following**
sentences and underline the Spanish words that are used in English.

Es una casa de adobe.
En el centro de la casa
   hay un patio.

E **Underline the correct completion to this sentence.**

                    una casa pequeña.

Hay muchos cuartos en

                    una casa grande.

F **What room are these people in? Match the activities with the rooms.**

   1. ____ José come.   **a.** el dormitorio, el cuarto de dormir

   2. ____ Elena toma un baño.   **b.** el comedor

   3. ____ Roberto duerme.   **c.** el cuarto de baño

16 Mi familia

A **Tell about your family. If you do not have one of the relatives, put an X in the blank.**

1. Yo tengo _____ hermanos.

2. Yo tengo _____ hermanas.

3. Yo tengo _____ primos (y primas).

4. Yo tengo _____ tías.

5. Yo tengo _____ tíos.

B **Choose the correct words to complete the following dictionary.**

| tío | primo | hermano | abuelo |
| tía | prima | hermana | abuela |

1. _____ : un hermano de mi padre o madre

2. _____ : otro hijo de mi madre o padre

3. _____ : la madre de mi madre o padre

4. _____ : una hija de mi tío o tía

5. _____ : el padre de mi madre o padre

C **Something is funny about the dictionary in Activity B. A dictionary always has the words in alphabetical order. Arrange the words in alphabetical order.**

1. _____

2. _____

3. _____

4. _____

5. _____

WELCOME TO SPANISH

D **See how easy it is to guess the meaning of words. Choose the correct word to complete each sentence.**

1. El padre de mi padre es mi abuelo _____. (materno, paterno)

2. El padre de mi madre es mi abuelo _____. (materno, paterno)

E **Underline the correct ending of this sentence.**

                                        una familia pequeña.
Hay muchas personas en
                                        una familia grande.

F **Complete the following with *tienes, tengo, tiene,* and any other words you may need. Then give true answers about yourself.**

1. ¿ _____ (tú) una familia grande o pequeña?

Yo _____ una familia _____ .

Hay _____ personas en mi familia.

2. ¿ _____ hermanos?

Sí, yo _____ _____ hermanos.

(o) No, yo no _____ hermanos.

3. Si tú _____ hermanos, ¿cuántos hermanos _____ ?

Yo _____ _____ hermanos.

4. ¿Cuántos años _____ ?

¿Yo? Yo _____ _____ años.

5. Y tu hermano, ¿cuántos años _____ ?

Él _____ _____ años.   (o)   Yo no _____

hermano.

6. Y tu hermana, ¿cuántos años _____ ?

Ella _____ _____ años.   (o)   Yo no _____ hermana.

G **Work with a classmate. Make up a story using the information from Activity F. Tell your stories to each other.**

17 Mi mascota

A On a separate sheet of paper, draw a picture of a pet store. Then work with a classmate and have a conversation about buying a pet. Use a separate sheet of paper for your drawing.

B Write *sí* after each true sentence and *no* after each false one.

1. Un canario es un pájaro. ____

2. Un gerbo es un pájaro también. ____

3. Un perro es un animal doméstico. ____

4. Un elefante es un animal doméstico también. ____

5. Un tigre es un animal salvaje. ____

6. Un león es de la misma familia que un gato. ____

7. Una víbora es un reptil. ____

8. Un pez dorado es un reptil también. ____

C Answer these questions about yourself.

1. ¿Te interesa la historia?

_____

2. ¿Te gusta la clase de historia?

_____

3. ¿Te gusta mucho o un poco?

_____

4. ¿Te interesan las matemáticas?

_____

5. ¿Te gusta la clase de matemáticas?

_____

_____

WELCOME TO SPANISH

6. ¿Te gusta mucho o un poco?

_____

D **Complete these sentences with *-a* or *-an*.**

Me gust____ los animales. Me gust____ mucho. Yo tengo una mascota.

Tengo un perro. Me encant____ mi perro. Es adorable.

Yo tengo un acuario también. En mi acuario hay pececillos.

Los pececillos me interes____ mucho.

E **Match the activity in the picture with the word.**

a. salta   **b.** juega   **c.** nada   **d.** canta   **e.** habla

1. ____   **2.** ____   **3.** ____

4. ____

5. ____

F **Complete the following sentences.**

1. El canario canta y yo cant____ también.

2. El perro salt____ y yo salt____ también.

3. El pececillo nad____ y yo nad____ también.

4. El papagayo habl____ y yo habl____ también.

5. El gato jueg____ y yo jueg____ también.

18 **L**os deportes

A Place the number where it belongs in the illustration.

1. el campo   **2.** el jugador
3. el balón   **4.** el equipo

B Complete the following words.

1. el vóli_____   **2.** el béis_____

3. el fút_____   **4.** el básquet_____

C Here are some words used in talking about sports. Can you guess what they mean? Tell which sport they go with.

a. el béisbol   **b.** el tenis   **c.** el fútbol

1. ____ el gol   **2.** ____ el foul   **3.** ____ el bate

4. ____ el pícher   **5.** ____ el jonrón   **6.** ____ la base

7. ____ la raqueta

D **Write *sí* after each true sentence and *no* after each false one.**

1. El pícher es un jugador de béisbol. _____

2. El béisbol es un deporte muy popular en los Estados Unidos. _____

3. El jugador de fútbol juega béisbol. _____

4. Hay once jugadores en el equipo de fútbol. _____

5. El jugador de tenis o el tenista juega con una raqueta. _____

6. Hay cien jugadores en un equipo de básquetbol. _____

E **Answer these questions about yourself.**

1. ¿Te gustan los deportes?

_____

2. ¿Te gusta el béisbol?

_____

3. ¿Te gusta el fútbol?

_____

4. ¿Te gusta el básquetbol?

_____

5. ¿Qué deporte te gusta más?

_____

19 La ropa

A Draw a person. Then label his or her clothing.

B Put an X by the clothing items that both boys and girls can wear.

1. los tenis   ____

2. la falda   ____

3. la sudadera   ____

4. el pantalón   ____

5. la blusa   ____

6. el blue jean   ____

C **Answer these questions about yourself.**

1. ¿Tienes un par de tenis?

_____

2. ¿Llevas los tenis a la escuela?

_____

3. ¿Tienes una sudadera?

_____

4. ¿Llevas la sudadera en el gimnasio?

_____

5. ¿Tienes un gorro?

_____

6. ¿Llevas el gorro en la sala de clase?

_____

Notice that you will hear both *el gorro* and *la gorra*.
el gorro   la gorra

A **L**et's Read in Spanish!

A You'll be surprised at how much Spanish you are able to read. Let's give it a try and find out how easy it really is.

España

España es un país. Está en el continente de Europa. España y Portugal forman una península—la península ibérica. Es una península porque tiene agua a los tres lados. Al este y al sur está el mar Mediterráneo. Al oeste está el océano Atlántico.

Los Pirineos están al norte. Los Pirineos son montañas altas. Las montañas forman una frontera natural entre España y Francia.

La capital de España es Madrid. Madrid está en el centro del país. Barcelona es otra ciudad importante de España. Barcelona es una ciudad industrial.

B Words that look alike and sound alike in two languages are called cognates. There are many cognates in this reading selection. Match the following cognates.

1. ____ continente   **a.** mountains

2. ____ península   **b.** form

3. ____ Europa   **c.** industrial

4. ____ forman   **d.** important

5. ____ este   **e.** peninsula

6. ____ norte   **f.** center

7. ____ océano   **g.** ocean

8. ____ montañas   **h.** Europe

9. ____ importante   **i.** frontier (border)

10. ____ frontera   **j.** east

11. ____ industrial   **k.** north

12. ____ centro   **l.** continent

C **Choose the correct completion to each statement.**

1. España es _____.

   a. un continente   **b.** un país   **c.** una península

2. España y _____ forman una península.

   a. Francia   **b.** Barcelona   **c.** Portugal

3. _____ tiene agua a los tres lados.

   a. Una península   **b.** Un país   **c.** Un continente

4. _____ es la capital de España.

   a. Barcelona   **b.** Madrid   **c.** Sevilla

5. El Mediterráneo es _____.

   a. un mar   **b.** un océano   **c.** una montaña

B Reading about Science

A **Read the following passage about biology. You'll be amazed how easy it is.**

La biología es una ciencia. Es la ciencia que estudia las plantas y los animales. El biólogo es el científico que estudia la biología. El biólogo o la bióloga trabaja en un laboratorio. Para sus investigaciones usa un microscopio. En el microscopio observa y estudia células, bacteria y virus.

B **In the reading selection, find a word that is related to each of the following words.**

1. el biólogo _____

2. la ciencia _____

3. el estudio _____

4. la observación _____

5. celular _____

6. viral _____

Welcome to *French!*

Les salutations

A Circle the letter of the best response.

1. Salut!
   a. Merci.
   b. Ça va bien.
   c. Salut!

2. Ça va?
   a. Ça va.
   b. Et toi?
   c. Salut!

3. Ça va. Et toi?
   a. Et toi?
   b. Ça va?
   c. Ça va bien, merci.

B In the illustrations below, which people are probably saying *Salut* and which are probably saying *Bonjour?* Write A for those saying *Salut!* and B for those saying *Bonjour.*

1. _____

2. _____

3. _____

C Just as English speakers use abbreviations, French speakers also abbreviate words. Here are few examples:

Monsieur	M.
Madame	Mme
Mademoiselle	Mlle

Note that the abbreviation "Ms." does not exist in French.

Address the envelopes to the following people in French using abbreviations.

    1. Miss Briand
    2. Mr. Benoît
    3. Mrs. Chandelier

D **Circle the expressions that have approximately the same meaning.**

    1. Ça va.
    2. Salut!
    3. Ça va bien.
    4. Bien, merci.
    5. Et toi?
    6. Pas mal!

Les salutations   **39**

WELCOME TO FRENCH

2 Au revoir

A **Decide who's saying what. Write the appropriate letter next to the illustration.**

a. Au revoir.   **b.** Ciao.   **c.** Salut!

1. ____

2. ____

3. ____

B **Choose the farewell you are going to use in each of the following situations. Write the letter that corresponds to the expression you choose.**

a. Au revoir.   **b.** Ciao.
c. À bientôt.   **d.** À demain.

1. You're saying "goodbye" to someone you plan to see tomorrow. ____

2. You're saying "goodbye" to an adult who's about to leave on a trip. ____

3. You're saying "so long" to a good friend. ____

4. You're saying "bye" to someone you plan on seeing again soon. ____

C **Look at the "farewells" in Activity B. Which one means almost the same thing as *À tout à l'heure?***

_____

WELCOME TO FRENCH

3 ❦ En classe

A **Match the word with the picture.**

a. une calculatrice   **b.** un crayon   **c.** une table

d. une feuille de papier   **e.** un ordinateur   **f.** une chaise

g. un stylo-bille   **h.** un livre

1. _____
2. _____
3. _____
4. _____
5. _____
6. _____
7. _____
8. _____

B **Write the missing letter in each word.**

un ____rayon   une t____ble   une c____aise

un pup____tre   une calculatric____   un liv____e

Now put the missing letters together to form a word. _____

C **Choose the items you need.**

a. une feuille de papier   **f.** une calculatrice
b. un livre   **g.** un ordinateur
c. un sac à dos   **h.** un morceau de craie
d. un crayon   **i.** une table
e. une gomme

1. _____ You are going to write a composition for your Language Arts class.

2. _____ You have lots of books and things to carry to school.

3. _____ You want to spread out materials to do a drawing.

4. _____ You are going to write something on the blackboard.

5. _____ You are going to solve an arithmetic problem with the help
            of a machine.

6. _____ You are going to do an arithmetic problem without a machine.

D **Write the missing letters in each word.**

1. un cah_____

2. un morc_____ de cr_____

3. une ch_____ se

4. une f_____ lle de pap_____

5. un ordinat_____

4 ❖ *Les nombres*

A Write the number.

1. trois _____

2. treize _____

3. trente _____

4. trois cents _____

5. trois cent trois _____

6. trois mille _____

7. six _____

8. seize _____

9. soixante-six _____

10. six cents _____

11. six cent soixante _____

12. six mille _____

13. huit _____

14. dix-huit _____

15. quatre-vingts _____

16. quatre-vingt-huit _____

17. huit cents _____

18. huit cent quatre-vingt-huit _____

B Write the following famous years in American and French history.

1. dix-sept cent soixante-seize _____

2. quatorze cent quatre-vingt-douze _____

3. dix-sept cent quatre-vingt-neuf _____

Les nombres

Match the historical event with the year indicated above.

1. l'arrivé de Christophe Colomb au nouveau monde _____

2. l'indépendance des États-Unis d'Amérique _____

3. la Révolution Française _____

C **Write the letter next to the name of the money.**

a. cent euros français
b. cinquante euros français
c. vingt euros français

1. _____

2. _____

3. _____

5 La politesse

A Who's saying what? Write the letter in the space provided.

a. Je vous en prie.

b. Merci.

1. ____

2. ____

B You're in a café ordering something to drink. You want to be polite. Choose the correct completion to your statement.

1. Un coca, ____.
a. merci
b. je vous en prie
c. s'il vous plaît

2. C'est combien le coca, ____?
a. merci
b. je vous en prie
c. s'il vous plaît

C Choose the expressions being used between the speakers in each picture.

a. Je vous en prie.   **b.** Je t'en prie.
c. S'il vous plaît.   **d.** S'il te plaît.

1. ____   2. ____

D Look at this menu from a French café. Work with a classmate. Each of you will decide what you are going to order.

L'Affaire

Soupe à l'oignon	5€
Salade verte	5€
Pâté	7€
Pizza	9€
Spaghetti	8€
Omelette	8€
Sandwich au fromage	6€
Sandwich au jambon	7€
Sandwich au poulet	7€
Steak frites	10€
Crêpe	6€
Tarte aux fruits	6€
Glace au chocolat	4€
Sorbet	4€

6 **L'heure**

A **Match the time with each clock.**

    a. Il est une heure.

    b. Il est deux heures trente. Il est deux heures et demie.

    c. Il est sept heures quarante.

    d. Il est dix heures quinze.

    e. Il est trois heures vingt.

    f. Il est onze heures trente-cinq.

1. ____   2. ____   3. ____

4. ____   5. ____   6. ____

B **Write out the time for each event.**

    1. Le concert est à deux heures et demie. _____

    2. Le film est à huit heures quarante. _____

    3. Le dîner est à sept heures trente. _____

    4. Le show commence à huit heures quinze. _____

7 Les couleurs

A What colors would you need to color the sky, the clouds, and the grass in a picture of a park on a beautiful spring day? Answer in French.

_____

B Color this bird in at least three colors and label them in French.

_____

C The French and American flags are the same colors. The colors, however, are given in reverse order when describing the flags. When we describe the American flag, we say it is red, white, and blue. The French say their flag is blue, white, and red. Based on this information, complete the following sentences correctly.

1. Le drapeau américain est _____, _____ et _____.

2. Le drapeau français est _____, _____ et _____.

8 ◆ Les jours de la semaine

A **Write the missing letter of each word.**

____ercredi

s____medi

vend____edi

lun____i

jeud____

Now put together the missing letters to spell the day of the week in French.

_____

B **In English, the days of the week are written with a capital letter. In French, they are written with a small letter:** *lundi, mardi, mercredi, jeudi, vendredi, samedi, dimanche.* **Write a capital "A" next to the expression that means "capital letter," and a small "a" next to the expression that means "small letter".**

une lettre majuscule ____

une lettre minuscule ____

C **Read the following.**

Il y a sept jours dans une semaine. Les jours de la semaine sont lundi, mardi, mercredi, jeudi, vendredi, samedi et dimanche.

In French, the expression *huit jours* refers to a week. *Quinze jours* refers to two weeks. If there are seven days in a week, explain why French speakers refer to the week as having eight days and two weeks as having fifteen days.

_____

_____

_____

_____

_____

Les jours de la semaine **49**

❖9❖ Les mois et les saisons

A Complete the answers to the following questions.

1. Il y a combien de mois dans une année?

Il y a _____ mois dans une année.

2. Il y a combien de jours dans une semaine?

Il y a _____ jours dans une semaine.

3. Il y a combien de saisons dans une année?

Il y a _____ saisons dans une année.

B Choose the correct months.

1. ____ les mois d'hiver

2. ____ les mois du printemps

3. ____ les mois d'été

4. ____ les mois d'automne

a. juin, juillet et août   **b.** mars, avril et mai
c. décembre, janvier et février   **d.** septembre, octobre et novembre

C Complete each statement with the appropriate months.

1. Il y a 28 jours au mois de _____.

2. Il y a 30 jours aux mois d'_____.

3. Et il y a trente et un jours aux mois de_____.

D **Complete with true information.**

Mon anniversaire est au mois

de _____ (au mois d' ____).

La date de mon anniversaire c'est le _____.

E **Answer the following questions according to the calendar.**

lundi	mardi	mercredi	jeudi	vendredi	samedi	dimanche
31	1	2	3	4	5	6

1. Aujourd'hui c'est quel jour?

_____

2. Et demain, c'est quel jour?

_____

F **Write in French the months and seasons when people do these activities.**

1. le baseball _____

_____

2. le football _____

_____

3. le ski _____

_____

10 Le temps

A **Write the number of the sentence next to the picture that goes with it.**

1. Il neige.　　　**2.** Il fait très froid.　　　**3.** Il fait chaud.
4. Il y a du soleil.　　**5.** Il y a du vent.

a. _____

b. _____

c. _____

e. _____

d. _____

B **Circle the letter of the expressions that can be used to support the numbered sentences. There may be more than one answer.**

1. Il fait beau.
  a. Il pleut.
  b. Il y a du soleil.
  c. Il fait chaud.
  d. Il neige.
  e. Il y a du vent.

2. Il fait mauvais.
  a. Il pleut.
  b. Il neige.
  c. Il y a du soleil.
  d. Il fait très, très froid.
  e. Il fait un temps splendide.

Je suis...

A **Circle the correct choice.**

1. A French person uses _____ when speaking about himself or herself.
  a. tu   **b.** je

2. A French person uses _____ when addressing or talking to a friend.
  a. tu   **b.** je

B **Complete the following conversations with *tu es* or *je suis*.**

1. —Salut! _____ _____ une amie de Jean Paul, n'est-ce pas?

—Oui, _____ _____ une amie de Jean Paul.

_____ _____ Thérèse Lepoint.

2. —Salut! _____ _____ un ami de Serge, n'est-ce pas?

—Oui. _____ _____ un ami de Serge.

_____ _____ Hervé. Et toi?

—_____ _____ Nathalie Dumas, n'est-ce pas?

C After you complete the conversations in Activity B, get together with a classmate. Perform the conversations together.

D Answer the following question.

Tu t'appelles comment?

Je m'appelle _____.

E You will notice as you study French that many words are spelled differently, even though they are pronounced the same. Two examples are:

un ami   une amie

1. Underline the correct completion to each statement.
   a. *Une amie* refers to a (girl, boy).
   b. *Un ami* refers to a (girl, boy).

2. Complete each sentence.

   a. Robert est _____ _____ de Jean-Claude.

   b. Émilie est _____ _____ de Jean-Claude aussi.

WELCOME TO FRENCH

12 Je suis de...

A **Circle the appropriate completions to the following conversations.**

1. —Tu es d'où, Charles?
—Moi, je suis de Paris.
Ah, tu es _____. (français, américain)

2. —Tu es d'où, Carole?
—Moi, je suis de New York.
Ah, tu es _____. (française, américaine)

B **Select the correct question word and write it in the blank.**

Qui   *D'où*

—_____ est un ami de Christian?

—Robert.

—Il est _____, Robert?

—Robert est de New York.

—Ah, il est américain.

C **Complete the following words with *e* when necessary.**

1. Nathalie est français____.

2. Et Paul est français____ aussi.

3. Robert est américain____.

4. Et Susanne est américain____ aussi.

5. Susanne est une ami____ de Robert.

6. Et Robert est un ami____ de Nathalie et Paul.

7. Moi, je suis américain____.

13 *Je parle français*

A Look at this map. French is the language spoken in each of these countries. How many of the capitals listed below can you match with their country?

1. Bamako   _____

2. Bruxelles   _____

3. Rabat   _____

4. Abidjan   _____

5. Dakar   _____

6. Paris   _____

7. Tunis   _____

B **Choose the correct question word to complete each statement.**

Qui   *D'où*

1. —_____ parle français?

—Michel parle français.

—Ah oui? Il est _____?

—Michel est de Marseille.

2. —_____ parle italien?

—Gianni parle italien.

—Ah oui?

—Oui, il est de Venise.

—Il est_____?

—De Venise.

3. —_____ parle anglais?

—Annette parle anglais.

—Ah, oui. Elle est de New York,

n'est-ce pas?

—Non.

—Elle est _____, alors?

—Annette est de Boston.

Je parle français   **57**

D Find the names of the languages in the following puzzle. Circle each language you find. The name can be read from left to right, right to left, top to bottom, bottom to top, or diagonally.

```
J  A  P  O  N  A  I  S  O  Q  F  P  A  J
N  K  O  N  S  U  B  Y  T  Z  L  S  C  A
T  V  R  S  E  L  W  B  O  T  C  I  E  R
W  I  T  A  L  I  E  N  G  W  Q  A  S  M
E  V  U  R  D  X  M  K  S  P  H  D  S  T
K  I  G  T  P  N  Z  A  U  D  É  N  U  S
S  I  A  Ç  N  A  R  F  N  E  B  A  R  A
I  Q  I  G  M  N  D  T  Z  T  R  L  J  V
O  E  S  P  A  G  N  O  L  K  E  R  D  P
N  R  Z  S  P  L  P  M  X  F  U  I  D  Z
I  R  C  S  I  A  N  O  L  O  P  G  V  R
H  W  U  R  Y  I  Z  E  V  T  K  O  Q  X
C  E  R  G  B  S  U  P  Z  R  D  K  E  I
```

Word Bank

grec	portugais	hébreu
chinois	polonais	italien
arabe	anglais	français
vietnamien	espagnol	
japonais	russe	

When you have completed the puzzle, use the bold letters to form a French word.

___ ___ ___ ___ ___

14 J'aime...

A **Match the subject with the book cover.**

   a. le latin   **b.** l'histoire   **c.** la biologie

   d. la musique   **e.** la géographie   **f.** l'art

1. ____

2. ____

3. ____

4. ____

5. ____

6. ____

B **Complete each of the following words with the missing letters.**

   1. l'ar____   **2.** le françai____   **3.** l'anglai____   **4.** le moi____

   5. juille____   **6.** chau____   **7.** mauvai____   **8.** je sui____

C Now pronounce the words from Activity B. Notice that the letters that you added are not pronounced. As you learn to spell in French, you will note that there are many letters that are not pronounced.

D List the classes you like and don't like.

1. J'aime _____.

2. Je n'aime pas _____.

E Complete the following sentences with the negative.

1. Je suis américain(e). Je _____ suis _____ français(e).

2. Je parle français. Je _____ parle _____ espagnol.

3. Il fait chaud. Il _____ fait _____ froid.

4. Il neige. Il _____ pleut _____.

F Complete the following sentences with the negative.

1. Jean est français. Il _____ est _____ américain.

2. Jean est de Nice. Il _____ est _____ de Paris.

3. Jean aime les maths. Il _____ aime _____ la biologie.

4. Moi, j'aime _____. Je _____ aime _____ _____.

WELCOME TO FRENCH

NAME _____   DATE _____

15 Ma maison

A **Label the rooms of this house.**

1. le salon   2. la cuisine   3. la chambre
4. la salle à manger 5. la salle de bains

B **Indicate if the following statements are *vrai* (V) or *faux* (F).**

1. _____ Il y a une voiture dans le garage.

2. _____ Il y a un jardin autour de la maison

3. _____ Il y a vingt pièces dans la maison.

4. _____ Il y a des roses dans le jardin.

Ma maison   **61**

C Choose the correct word to complete each sentence.

petite   *grande*

Il y a quatre pièces dans une _____ maison. Il y a douze pièces

dans une_____ maison.

D Guess what room Jean-Claude is in.

la cuisine   *la salle à manger*   *la salle de bains*   *le garage*

1. Jean-Claude is working on his car.   _____

2. Jean-Claude is preparing a sandwich.   _____

3. Jean-Claude is having dinner.   _____

4. Jean-Claude is taking a shower.   _____

16 Ma famille

A Circle the statement that is true for you.

1. **a.** J'ai un frère.
   b. J'ai des frères.
   c. Je n'ai pas de frère.

2. **a.** J'ai une soeur.
   b. J'ai des soeurs.
   c. Je n'ai pas de soeur.

3. **a.** J'ai un cousin.
   b. J'ai des cousins.
   c. Je n'ai pas de cousin.

4. **a.** J'ai une tante.
   b. J'ai des tantes.
   c. Je n'ai pas de tante.

B Tell about your family and relatives. If you do not have any, put an X in the blank.

1. J'ai _____ (frère, frères).

2. J'ai _____ (soeur, soeurs).

3. J'ai _____ (cousin, cousins).

4. J'ai _____ (oncle, oncles).

5. J'ai _____ (tante, tantes).

C Answer the following questions about yourself.

1. Tu as une grande famille ou une petite famille?

_____

2. Il y a combien de personnes dans ta famille?

_____

3. Tu as une grande maison ou une petite maison?

_____

4. Il y a combien de pièces dans ta maison?

_____

D See how easy it is to guess the meaning of words. Circle the correct word to complete each statement.

    1. Le père de mon père est mon grand-père _____ .(maternel, paternel)

    2. Le père de ma mère est mon grand-père _____. (maternel, paternel)

E Complete the following sentences with *as, ai,* or *a.* Then give true answers about yourself.

    1. Tu _____ une grande famille ou une petite famille?

    Moi, j'_____ une _____ famille.

    Il y a _____ personnes dans ma famille.

    2. Tu _____ des frères?

    Oui, j'_____ des frères. (ou) Non, je n'_____ pas de frère.

    3. Tu _____ quel âge?

    Moi, j'_____ _____ ans.

    4. Et ton frère? Il _____ quel âge?

    Mon frère _____ _____ ans. (ou) Je n'_____ pas de frère.

    5. Et ta soeur? Elle _____ quel âge?

    Ma soeur _____ _____ ans. (ou) Moi, je n'_____ pas de soeur.

F Work with a classmate. Make up a story using the information from Activity E. Tell your story to each other.

WELCOME TO FRENCH

17 Un bon ami

A On a separate sheet of paper, draw a picture of a pet store. Then work with a classmate and have a conversation together about buying a pet.

B Indicate if the following statements are *vrai* (V) or *faux* (F).

1. ____ Le canari est un oiseau.

2. ____ La gerboise est un oiseau aussi.

3. ____ Le chien est un animal domestique.

4. ____ L'éléphant est un autre animal domestique.

5. ____ Le tigre est un animal sauvage.

6. ____ Le lion est de la même famille que le chat.

7. ____ Un serpent est un reptile.

8. ____ Un poisson rouge est un reptile aussi.

C Match the activity in the picture with the word.

a. il chante   **b.** il nage   **c.** elle parle   **d.** il saute

1. ____

2. ____

3. ____

4. ____

D Choose the correct animal to complete each statement and write it in the blank.

     le chat   *la perruche*   *le poisson*   *le canari*

1. _____ chante.

2. _____ parle.

3. _____ saute.

4. _____ nage.

E Fill in the missing letters to complete the word for an animal.

1. ____anari

2. perruc____e

3. ois____au

4. gerbo____se

5. serpe____t

Now use the letters to spell the name of an animal.

     _____

18 Les sports

A **Place the number where it belongs in the illustration.**

1. le terrain
2. le joueur
3. l'équipe
4. le ballon

B **Rewrite the following words in their shortened forms.**

1. le foot(ball) _____

2. le volley(-ball) _____

3. le basket(-ball) _____

C **Here are some words related to sports. Can you guess what they mean? Indicate the sports with which they are associated.**

a. le base(-ball)   **b.** le foot(ball)   **c.** le tennis

1. la défense _____

2. le bâton _____

3. le serveur _____

4. la raquette _____

5. l'attaque _____

D **Tell if the following statements about sports are *vrai* (V) or *faux* (F).**

1. _____ Le foot est un sport d'équipe.

2. _____ Le baseball est un sport individuel. Il n'y a pas d'équipe.

3. _____ Il y a onze joueurs dans une équipe de football.

4. _____ Il y a cent joueurs dans une équipe de basketball.

19 Les vêtements

A On a separate sheet of paper, draw a person. Draw his or her clothing. Then label what he or she is wearing.

B Put an X by the clothes that boys and girls can wear.

1. les tennis _____   **2.** un pantalon _____

3. un (blue) jean _____   **4.** une blouse _____

5. un pull _____   **6.** une jupe _____

7. un blouson _____   **8.** une casquette _____

C Answer these questions about yourself.

1. Tu as une paire de tennis?

_____

2. Tu portes les tennis à l'école?

_____

3. Tu as un sweat-shirt?

_____

4. Tu portes un sweat-shirt au gymnase?

_____

5. Tu as une casquette?

_____

6. Tu portes une casquette en classe?

_____

_____

Let's Read in French!

A **You will be surprised at how much French you are able to read.
Let's give it a try and find out how easy it really is.**

La France

L'Europe est un continent. La France est un pays. La France est en Europe. Paris est la capitale de la France. Il y a beaucoup de monuments fameux à Paris—la tour Eiffel, le Louvre, Notre Dame.

Lille est une ville importante de la France. Lille est une ville industrielle. Il y a beaucoup d'industrie à Lille.

Il y a des montagnes en France. Les Alpes sont dans l'est et les Pyrénées sont dans le sud.

B **Words that look alike and sound alike in both languages are cognates. Find the French cognate for the following words.**

1. Europe _____

2. capital _____

3. continent _____

4. monument _____

5. east _____

6. mountains _____

7. important _____

8. industrial _____

C **Choose the correct completion to each statement.**

1. La France est _____.
   a. un continent   **b.** un pays   **c.** une péninsule

2. Les Pyrénées sont des _____.
   a. montagnes   **b.** lacs   **c.** mers

3. Lille est une ville _____.
   a. industrielle   **b.** pittoresque   **c.** tropicale

4. La tour Eiffel est _____ de Paris.
   a. une montagne   **b.** une ville   **c.** un monument

Let's Read in French! **69**

Reading about Biology

A **Read the following passage about biology. You'll be amazed how easy it is.**

La biologie est une science. La biologie est la science qui étudie les plantes et les animaux. Un biologiste ou une biologiste étudie la biologie. Un (une) biologiste travaille dans un laboratoire. Il (Elle) utilise un microscope pour faire des recherches. Dans le microscope il (elle) observe, étudie et analyse les cellules, les bactéries et les virus.

B **Read this selection once again and find all the cognates.**

_____

_____

_____

_____

C **Many words are related to one another because they come from the same root. For example, the words _la biologie_ and _le (la) biologiste_ are related. In the reading selection, find words that are related to the following.**

1. un biologiste _____

2. une étude _____

3. une observation _____

4. cellulaire _____

5. bactérien _____

6. viral _____

Welcome to Italian!

Ciao!

A Look at the two illustrations. Write A or B to indicate in which conversation each expression is being used.

1. ____ Buon giorno.   2. ____ Come stai?

3. ____ Come sta?   4. ____ Ciao!

5. ____ Bene, grazie. E tu?   6. ____ Bene, grazie. E Lei?

A.

B.

B Circle the letter of the best response.

1. Ciao!   2. Come stai?   3. Buon giorno.
   a. Ciao!   a. Bene, grazie. E Lei?   a. Grazie. E Lei?
   b. E tu?   b. Bene, grazie. E tu?   b. Buon giorno.
   c. Grazie.   c. Ciao, grazie.   c. Buona sera.

C Number the following in order from "so-so" to "really great, fabulous."

____ Abbastanza bene.   ____ Benissimo.

____ Così, così.   ____ Bene.

____ Molto bene.

2 *Arrivederci!*

A **Choose the correct responses you would use in taking leave of someone.**

1. an older person you hardly know
   a. Ciao!
   b. Ci vediamo.
   c. ArriverLa.

2. a close friend your own age
   a. Ciao!
   b. ArriverLa.
   c. Arrivederci.

3. someone you're going to see again the same day
   a. A domani.
   b. Arrivederci.
   c. A più tardi.

4. someone you're going to see again really soon
   a. A presto.
   b. Arrivederci.
   c. ArriverLa.

5. someone you plan to see again tomorrow
   a. A più tardi.
   b. A domani.
   c. Ciao.

B **Complete the following words with the correct letters. Then pronounce the words carefully.**

1. Arriveder____ ____.

2. ____ ____ vediamo.

3. ____ ____ ao.

3 In classe

A **Match the word with the illustration.**

  a. una calcolatrice   **b.** una sedia   **c.** un quaderno
  d. una matita   **e.** una penna   **f.** un tavolo
  g. uno zaino   **h.** una gomma

1. ____

2. ____

3. ____

4. ____

5. ____

6. ____

7. ____

8. ____

B **Match the things that you usually use together.**

1. una matita e ____   **a.** una sedia

2. un foglio di carta e ____   **b.** una penna

3. un tavolo e ____   **c.** una gomma

C Underline the appropriate expression to be used when you receive a present or a favor from someone.

    1. Grazie.

    2. Come stai?

D Write the missing letter in each word.

    1. una ma____ita

    2. una penn____

    3. un ta____olo

    4. un libr____

    5. una ca____colatrice

    6. uno zain____

Now put the missing letters together to form a word. _____

E Circle the two expressions that mean the same thing in Italian.

    1. Cos'è?

    2. Come sta?

    3. Che cos'è?

WELCOME TO ITALIAN

4 Numeri

A **Write the number.**

1. tre _____

2. tredici _____

3. trenta _____

4. trentatré _____

5. trecento _____

6. trecentotrentatré _____

7. tremilatrecentotrentatré _____

B **Write the number.**

1. otto _____

2. diciotto _____

3. ottanta _____

4. cinque _____

5. quindici _____

6. cinquanta _____

7. nove _____

8. diciannove _____

9. novanta _____

C **Write the following famous years in American history.**

1. millequattrocentonovantadue _____

2. millesettecentosettantasei _____

D **Match the historical event with the year indicated above.**

1. _____ l'independenza degli Stati Uniti

2. _____ Cristoforo Colombo ha scoperto l'America.

5 Prego

A Put the expressions in the order in which they would be used.

1. ____ **a.** Prego.   2. ____ **a.** Per piacere.

____ **b.** Grazie.   ____ **b.** Grazie.

____ **c.** Per favore.   ____ **c.** Prego.

B Circle the letter of the expression that means the same thing.

1. Ciao!
   a. Buona sera!
   b. Buon giorno!
   c. Come stai?

2. Per favore.
   a. Grazie.
   b. Prego.
   c. Per piacere.

3. Arrivederci!
   a. Ci vediamo!
   b. Buon giorno!
   c. A domani!

C Look at the following list of foods. Indicate if each is something to eat, *Per mangiare* or to drink, *Per bere*.

	Per mangiare	Per bere
1. una limonata	_____	_____
2. un' insalata verde	_____	_____
3. un'aranciata	_____	_____
4. pasta	_____	_____
5. un caffè espresso	_____	_____
6. spinaci	_____	_____
7. un tè	_____	_____
8. una patata	_____	_____
9. un cappuccino	_____	_____
10. una bistecca	_____	_____

WELCOME TO ITALIAN

D Look at this menu in an Italian restaurant. Work with a classmate. Each of you will tell what you are going to order. If you aren't sure what something is, find out from someone in the class. For example, you can ask: *Che cos'è* _____ ? and find out if someone else can help.

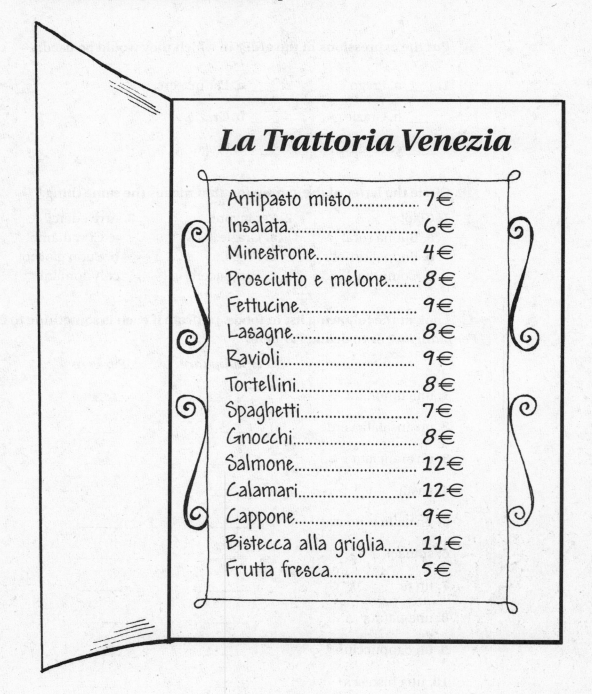

La Trattoria Venezia

Antipasto misto..............	7€
Insalata........................	6€
Minestrone.....................	4€
Prosciutto e melone........	8€
Fettucine.......................	9€
Lasagne........................	8€
Ravioli..........................	9€
Tortellini.......................	8€
Spaghetti......................	7€
Gnocchi........................	8€
Salmone........................	12€
Calamari.......................	12€
Cappone........................	9€
Bistecca alla griglia........	11€
Frutta fresca..................	5€

6 Che ora è?

A **Match the time with each clock.**

a. Sono le otto e mezzo.
b. Sono le dieci e venticinque.
c. È l'una e un quarto.
d. Sono le due e quarantacinque.
e. Sono le sei.
f. Sono le due e dieci.

1. ____
2. ____
3. ____

4. ____
5. ____
6. ____

B **Match the expressions that mean the same thing.**

1. ____ Sono le cinque e trenta.
a. Sono le cinque e un quarto.

2. ____ Sono le cinque e quindici.
b. Sono le sei meno venti.

3. ____ Sono le cinque e quaranta.
c. Sono le cinque e mezzo.

I _giorni della settimana_

A **Read the following and then complete the sentence.**

I giorni della settimana sono: lunedì, martedì, mercoledì, giovedì, venerdì, sabato e domenica.

Ci sono _____ giorni in una settimana.

B **Write the name of the day according to the calendar illustrated below.**

1. Che giorno è oggi? Oggi è _____.

2. E domani? _____.

lunedì	martedì	mercoledì	giovedì	venerdì	sabato	domenica
12	13	14	15	16	17	18

C **Write the missing letter in each word.**

1. lune____ì   **2.** merc____ledì   **3.** ____artedì

4. v____nerdì   **5.** lu____edì   **6.** g____ovedì

7. domeni____a   **8.** s____bato

Now put the missing letters together to spell a day of the week in Italian.

____ ____ ____ ____ ____ ____ ____

8 **M**esi e stagioni

A **Complete the following statements with Arabic numbers.**

1. Ci sono _____ mesi in un anno.

2. Ci sono _____ giorni in una settimana.

3. Ci sono _____ stagioni in un anno.

B **Match the months with their season.**

1. _____ i mesi dell'inverno   **a.** giugno, luglio e agosto

2. _____ i mesi della primavera   **b.** marzo, aprile e maggio

3. _____ i mesi dell'estate   **c.** dicembre, gennaio e febbraio

4. _____ i mesi dell'autunno   **d.** settembre, ottobre e novembre

C **Complete with true information.**

Il mio compleanno è il _____.

D **Answer the following questions according to the calendar illustrated below.**

novembre

			1	2	3	4
5	6	7	8	9	10	11
12	13	14	15	16	17	18
19	20	21	22	23	24	25
26	27	28	29	30		

Qual è la data di oggi?

_____

E **Complete the names of the following months with the correct letters.**

1. genn_____

2. febbr_____

3. magg_____

4. g_____gno

5. lugl_____

WELCOME TO ITALIAN

9 Il tempo

A Write the letter of the sentence next to the illustration that goes with it.

a. Nevica.   **b.** Fa molto freddo.   **c.** Fa caldo.
d. C'è sole.   **e.** Tira vento.

1. ____

2. ____

3. ____   **4.** ____   **5.** ____

B Circle the letter of the most appropriate response to each question.

1. Fa bel tempo oggi?
  a. Sì. Piove.
  b. Sono le due e mezzo.
  c. Sì. C'è sole.

2. Che tempo fa in dicembre?
  a. Fa molto caldo.
  b. Fa freddo e nevica.
  c. Così così.

3. Che tempo fa oggi?
  a. Bene, grazie.
  b. Fa brutto.
  c. Sono le tre e venticinque.

C Circle the weather expressions that mean the same thing.

1. a. Fa bello.
  b. Fa bel tempo.
  c. Fa brutto.

2. a. Fa cattivo tempo.
  b. Fa brutto.
  c. Fa bello.

WELCOME TO ITALIAN

Sono...

A **Circle the letter of the appropriate response.**

1. Sei americano, Ricardo?
   a. Sì, sei americano.
   b. Sì, sono americano.
   c. Sì, è americano.

2. Sei di Chicago?
   a. No, non sono di Chicago. Sono di Denver.
   b. No, non è di Chicago. È di Denver.
   c. No, non sei di Chicago. Sei di Denver.

3. Gianni è un amico di Graziana?
   a. Sì, sono un amico di Graziana.
   b. Sì, è un amico di Graziana.
   c. Sì, sei un amico di Graziana.

B **Complete the following conversation with *sei, sono,* or *è.***

—Anna Maria, _____ un'amica di Gianni Lombardi?

—Sì, io _____ un'amica di Gianni.

—_____ francese Gianni?

—No, non _____ francese. _____ italiano.

—Anche tu _____ italiana, non è vero?

—Sì, _____ italiana.

C **Complete the following with *-o* or *-a.***

Anna Maria è un'amic____ molto buon____. Anna Maria non è

american____. È italian____. E Marco è un amic____ molto buon____.

Marco non è italian____. Marco è american____.

Parlo italiano

A Complete each dialogue by adding the correct endings. Then work with a classmate to ask and answer the questions together.

1. —Tu parl____ russo?

—Io? No! Non parl____ russo.

—No?

—Io, no. Ma Svetlana parla russo.

2. —Parl____ inglese?

—Chi? Io?

—Sì, tu.

—Sì, parl____ inglese. Parl____ anche l'italiano.

B Find the names of languages in the following puzzle. Circle each language you find. The name can be read from left to right, right to left, top to bottom, bottom to top, or diagonally.

```
C  I  N  O  L  T  E  P  R  L  R
I  T  F  T  I  E  S  O  O  U  R
E  A  R  R  N  S  E  T  I  T  A
S  L  A  R  A  E  N  S  N  R  B
E  I  N  N  E  N  O  O  G  I  Q
N  A  C  I  O  C  C  A  L  O  P
O  N  A  G  L  R  S  E  E  L  O
P  O  R  T  O  G  H  E  S  E  L
P  L  A  N  P  I  O  R  E  E  A
A  A  B  O  S  A  P  P  O  L  C
I  C  O  C  E  R  G  I  A  N  C
G  I  O  L  O  N  G  A  P  S  O
```

When you have completed the puzzle, use the bold letters to form a word. The letters spell the name of a person:

___ ___ ___ ___ ___

Then change one letter in the name to make a new word.

___ ___ ___ ___ ___

Use the new words in a sentence.

_____

_____ .

C **Note that many words that start with a capital letter in English do not have a capital letter in Italian.**

Days: lunedì, martedì
Months: gennaio, febbraio
Languages: italiano, francese

Complete the following sentences with the appropriate letter.

1. Oggi è ____enerdì.

2. È il primo di ____uglio.

3. Parlo ____nglese e ____taliano.

WELCOME TO ITALIAN

Welcome to LATIN!

Salvē et Valē

A **Choose the correct response.**

1. If you had to greet someone in front of the *Forum Rōmānum* during the time of the Romans, what would you say?
  a. Valē.   **b.** Salvē.

2. How would you say "good-bye" to someone?
  a. Valē.   **b.** Salvē.

B **Complete the following dialogue.**

2 Numerī

A **Give the correct numbers using Arabic numerals.**

1. ūnus _____   **5.** octō _____

2. ūndecim _____   **6** centum _____

3. sex _____   **7.** vīgintī _____

4. duo _____   **8.** mille _____

B **Match each Roman numeral with its Arabic equivalent.**

a. 22   **c.** 10   **e.** 20   **g.** 1010
b. 660   **d.** 110   **f.** 18   **h.** 66

1. ____ X   **4.** ____ XX   **7.** ____ XXII

2. _____ XVIII   **5.** ____ CX   **8.** ____ MX

3. ____ LXVI   **6.** ____ DCLX

C **Use Arabic numbers to write the Roman numerals found on this crypt.**

_____

D **Choose the correct word to complete each statement.**

unison	quadriplegic	decimal
unite	century	duet
triplicate	quarters	octet
trio	octave	sextet

1. A _____ is a group of three.

2. A _____ is a period of one hundred years.

3. The two of them sang a lovely _____.

4. All must come together as one and _____ for the same cause.

5. The whole can be divided into four _____.

6. When doing math, don't forget to put the _____ point

in the correct place.

7. The musical scale has eight notes. Eight notes make up an

_____.

8. An _____ is a group of eight. Eight singers, for example, form

an _____ and six singers form a _____.

9. A _____ is a person who has lost the use of all four limbs—both

legs and both arms.

10. All those in favor yelled in _____.

11. I need three copies, so please prepare this in _____.

WELCOME TO LATIN

Paulus et Clāra

A Indicate whether the following words refer to a male or a female.

	male	female			male	female
1. Claudia	____	____	2. Fabius	____	____
3. amīcus	____	____	4. discipula	____	____
5. amīca	____	____	6. alumnus	____	____
7. discipulus	____	____	8. alumna	____	____
9. Rōmānus	____	____	10. Rōmāna	____	____

B Complete these sentences with *-a* or *-us*.

1. Paulus discipul____ bon____ est.

2. Flavia discipul____ bon____ est.

3. Flavia est quoque amīc____ bon____.

4. Paulus est Rōmān____ et Flavia quoque Rōmān____ est.

C Change these statements to questions.

1. Est Paulus Rōmānus. _____

2. Paulus est discipulus Rōmānus. _____

3. Rōmāna Claudia est. _____

4. Est Claudia amīca bona. _____

D Match the opposites.

1. ____ magnus   **a.** valē

2. ____ bonus   **b.** malus

3. ____ salvē   **c.** parvus

WELCOME TO LATIN

Paulus et Clāra

4 Amīcī et Discipulī

A Complete the following sentences with the appropriate letter.

1. Fabius et Caesar sunt amīc_____.

2. Sunt amīc_____ bon_____.

3. Fabius et Caesar sunt quoque discipul_____.

4. Sunt discipul_____ bon_____.

5. Claudia et Anna sunt amīc_____.

6. Claudia et Anna sunt puell_____.

7. Puell_____ bon_____ amīc_____ sunt.

8. Claudia et Anna sunt quoque discipul_____ bon_____.

B Write the plural forms of the following words.

1. amīca bona _____

2. discipulus bonus _____

3. casa parva _____

4. villa magna _____

5. amīcus Rōmānus _____

6. alumnus et alumna _____

C **Write the following sentences in the plural. Make all the necessary changes.**

1. Paula est puella.

Paula et Claudia _____.

2. Claudia est amīca bona.

Paula et Claudia _____.

3. Cornēlius est discipulus Rōmānus.

Cornēlius et Augustus _____.

4. Cornēlius est discipulus bonus.

Cornēlius et Augustus _____.

D **Choose the correct question word, *Quis, Qui,* or *Quae,* to complete each question.**

1. _____ est amīcus bonus? **2.** _____ est discipula bona?
Augustus est amīcus bonus.   Minerva discipula bona est.

3. _____ sunt discipulī? **4.** _____ sunt puellae Rōmānae?
Caesar et Marcus sunt discipulī.   Anna et Flavia sunt puellae Rōmānae.

E **Identify the following.**

1. paenīnsula **2.** īnsula
3. īnsula parva **4.** paenīnsula magna

a. _____

b. _____

c. _____

d. _____

Amīcī et Discipulī

WELCOME TO LATIN

5 Amīcus amīcam videt

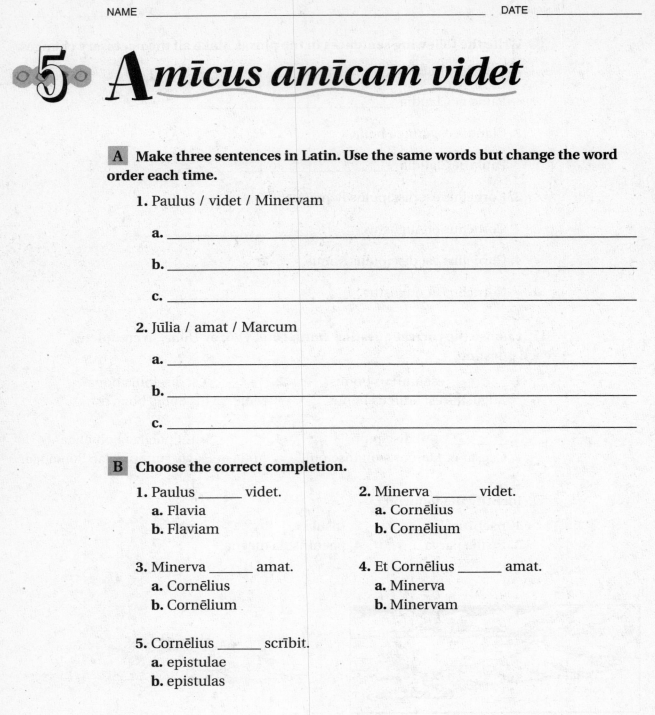

A Make three sentences in Latin. Use the same words but change the word order each time.

1. Paulus / videt / Minervam

   a. _____

   b. _____

   c. _____

2. Jūlia / amat / Marcum

   a. _____

   b. _____

   c. _____

B Choose the correct completion.

1. Paulus _____ videt.
   a. Flavia
   b. Flaviam

2. Minerva _____ videt.
   a. Cornēlius
   b. Cornēlium

3. Minerva _____ amat.
   a. Cornēlius
   b. Cornēlium

4. Et Cornēlius _____ amat.
   a. Minerva
   b. Minervam

5. Cornēlius _____ scrībit.
   a. epistulae
   b. epistulas

C Complete the following sentences with the correct endings.

1. Paulus, discipul_____ Rōmān_____, epistul_____ scrībit.

2. Livia, discipul_____ Rōmān_____, epistul_____ legit.

3. Paul_____ Livi_____ amat.

4. Paul_____ bon_____ amīc_____ Livi_____ amat.

5. Livi_____ Paul_____ amat.

6. Livi_____ bon_____ amīc_____ Paul_____ amat.

D Choose the correct question word, *Quis* or *Quem,* to complete each statement.

1. _____ est discipulus Rōmānus?

2. _____ amat discipulus Rōmānus?

3. _____ amat discipula Rōmāna?

WELCOME TO LATIN

Mottos in Latin

A Even today, Latin is used in many sayings and mottos. Here are some of the famous ones.

Veni, vidi, vici. I came, I saw, I conquered.
Uttered by Caesar after a short, brilliant military campaign.

Ne cede malis. Do not yield to misfortunes.
A quote from Virgil, the greatest Latin epic poet.

cum grano salis with a grain of salt
A quote from Pliny the Elder, famous Roman writer and military leader.

Carpe diem. Seize the day.
From the famous Roman lyric poet, Ovid.

Parvum parva decent. Small things become the small.
From Horace, the greatest of Rome's lyric poets.

Amicus est alter idem. A friend is a second self.
From Cicero's famous "Essay on Friendship".

Accipere quem facere iniuriam praestat.
It is better to suffer a wrong than to do one.
A quote from Cicero, Rome's greatest orator and person of letters.

Semper fidelis. Always faithful.
From the United States Marines.

State mottos:

North Carolina	**Melius esse quam videri.** Better to be than to seem.	
South Carolina	**Dum spiro, spero.** While I breathe, I hope.	
Arizona	**Deus ditat.** God enriches.	
Colorado	**Nil sine numine.** Nothing without divine guidance.	
Michigan	**Si quaeris peninsulam amoenan, circumspice.** If you are seeking a charming peninsula, look about you.	
Washington, D.C.	**Iustitia omnibus.** Justice to all.	
Oklahoma	**Labor omnia vincit.** Work conquers all.	

B Find out if your state's motto is in Latin. Chances are it is. What is the motto in Latin and what does it mean in English?

_____

_____

Welcome to GERMAN!

Begrüßung

A **Choose the correct completions to this conversation.**

1. a. Wie geht es Ihnen?
   b. Wie geht's?
2. a. dir
   b. mir
3. a. gut
   b. schlecht

B **In each of the following, circle the expression that is the more formal.**

1. a. Tag.   **b.** Guten Tag.
2. a. Wie geht's?   **b.** Wie geht es Ihnen?
3. a. Und Ihnen?   **b.** Und dir?

C **Match the conversation with the picture.**

1. —Tag, Erika.
    Tag, Dieter. Wie geht's?
   —Es geht. Und dir?
    Nicht schlecht, danke.

2. —Guten Tag, Frau Müller.
    Wie geht es Ihnen?
   —Es geht mir sehr gut, danke.
    Und Ihnen?
   —Sehr gut, danke.

WELCOME TO GERMAN

2 **V**erabschieden

A **Circle all the correct responses you would use in taking leave of someone.**

1. Wie geht's?   **2.** Tschüs.   **3.** Bis bald.

4. Sehr gut.   **5.** Bis morgen.   **6.** Danke.

7. Auf Wiedersehen.

B **Choose the expression you would use in each of the following situations.**

a. Auf Wiedersehen.   **b.** Bis später.   **c.** Bis gleich.

d. Bis morgen.   **e.** Tschüs.

1. ____ You're saying "good-bye" to a friend whom you expect to see again soon.

2. ____ You're saying "bye" to an older person who is leaving on a trip.

3. ____ You're saying "so long" to a close friend.

4. ____ You're saying "good-bye" to someone you expect to see again tomorrow.

5. ____ You're saying "bye" to someone you expect to see again fairly soon.

C **Match the following conversations with the pictures.**

1. —Tschüs, Ingrid.   **2.** —Wie geht's?
    —Tschau, Erik. Bis morgen.   —Sehr gut, danke. Und dir?
                                     —Gut auch.

a. ____   **b.** ____

WELCOME TO GERMAN

Verabschieden

3 **I**m Klassenzimmer

A **Match the word with the illustration.**

a. ein Buch   **b.** ein Kugelschreiber   **c.** ein Schreibtisch
d. ein Rucksack   **e.** eine Kreide   **f.** ein Rechner
g. ein Bleistift   **h.** ein Schwamm

1. _____

2. _____

3. _____

4. _____

5. _____

6. _____

7. _____

8. _____

B **Match the things that you usually use together.**

    a. Schwamm   **c.** Bleistift

    b. Tisch   **d.** Kugelschreiber

    1. der _____ und der Stuhl

    2. die Kreide und der _____

    3. ein Stück Papier und der _____ oder der _____

C **Write the missing letter.**

    1. der K____gelschreiber

    2. das He____t

    3. der ____lock

    4. der St____hl

    5. der Rechne____

    6. die Krei____e

D **Note that unlike English, all German nouns begin with a capital letter. Complete the following.**

    1. der ____ucksack

    2. der ____isch

    3. ein ____tück ____apier

    4. das ____uch

    5. der ____leistift

WELCOME TO GERMAN

Im Klassenzimmer   **101**

4 Die Zahlen

A Write the number.

1. eins   _____

2. elf   _____

3. einundzwanzig   _____

4. (ein)hundert   _____

5. drei   _____

6. dreizehn   _____

7. dreißig   _____

8. dreiunddreißig   _____

9. dreihundertdreiunddreißig   _____

10. dreitausend   _____

B Write the number.

1. zwölf   _____

2. fünfzehn   _____

3. achtzig   _____

4. fünfundsechzig   _____

5. achtundneunzig   _____

C Jot down the following telephone numbers.

Wie ist die Telefonnummer, bitte?

1. neun-drei-drei-fünf-vier-acht _____

2. dreiundneunzig-fünfunddreißig-achtundvierzig _____

3. zwölf-zweiundzwanzig-sechzig _____

4. fünfundachtzig-vierundsiebzig-dreizehn _____

WELCOME TO GERMAN

5 Umgangsformen

A Match the expression(s) with the illustration.

1. Eine Tasse Kaffee, bitte.
2. **a.** Danke sehr.
   b. Bitte schön.
3. **a.** Bitte.
   b. Danke.

B Look at this menu in a German restaurant. Work with a classmate. Each of you will tell what you are going to order. If you aren't sure what something is, find out from someone in the class. For example, you can ask: *Was ist das?* and find out if someone else can help.

Matterhorn

Salat	5€
Heringssalat	7€
Suppe	3€
Bratwurst	5€
Wienerschnitzel	10€
Sauerbraten mit Kartoffelkloß	13€
Apfelstrudel	5€
Pudding	4€
Karamelpudding	4€
Vanilleeis	2€

C Look at the names of the following foods in German. Can you guess what they are?

1. der Sellerie _____
2. der Brokkoli _____
3. der Apfel _____
4. die Wassermelone _____
5. das Filet Mignon _____
6. die Salami _____
7. die Tomate _____
8. der Thunfisch _____

Umgangsformen **103**

WELCOME TO GERMAN

⑥ **D**ie Uhrzeit

A **Match the time with each clock.**

a. Es ist elf Uhr fünf.   **b.** Es ist zwei Uhr zehn.
c. Es ist zehn Uhr.   **d.** Es ist sechs Uhr fünfundzwanzig.
e. Es ist halb neun.   **f.** Es ist vier Uhr vierzig.

1. _____   2. _____   3. _____

4. _____   5. _____   6. _____

7 Die Tage

A Note that the days of the week in German are capitalized the same as they are in English. Complete the following with the missing letters.

1. ____ontag

2. ____ienstag

3. ____ittwoch

4. ____onnerstag

5. ____reitag

6. ____amstag

7. ____onntag

B Answer based on the calendar.

Montag	Dienstag	Mittwoch	Donnerstag	Freitag	Samstag	Sonntag
28	29	30	1	2	3	4

1. Welcher Tag ist heute? _____

2. Und welcher Tag ist morgen? _____

C Explain in your own words why Wednesday is called *Mittwoch*.

_____

_____

_____

WELCOME TO GERMAN

Die Monate und die Jahreszeiten

A Write the missing letter to give the name of a month.

1. O____tober

2. De____ember

3. ____uli

4. Ma____

5. M____rz

B Some months in German are exactly the same as in English. Which ones are they?

_____

_____

_____

_____

C Complete the following statements.

1. Es gibt _____ Monate in einem Jahr.

2. Es gibt _____ Tage in einer Woche.

3. Es gibt _____ Jahreszeiten in einem Jahr.

D **Choose the correct months.**

1. ____ der Winter   **a.** März, April und Mai

2. ____ der Frühling   **b.** Dezember, Januar und Februar

3. ____ der Sommer   **c.** September, Oktober und November

4. ____ der Herbst   **d.** Juni, Juli und August

E **Complete the following sentences.**

1. Der _____ hat achtundzwanzig Tage.

2. Der _____, der _____, der _____, und

   der _____ haben dreißig Tage.

3. Der _____, der _____, der _____, der _____,

   der _____, der _____ und der _____ haben
   einunddreißig Tage.

WELCOME TO GERMAN

⑨ Das Wetter

A **Write the letter of the sentence next to the picture it describes.**

a. Es ist windig.   **b.** Es schneit.   **c.** Es ist sonnig.
d. Es regnet.   **e.** Es ist heiß.   **f.** Es ist sehr kalt.

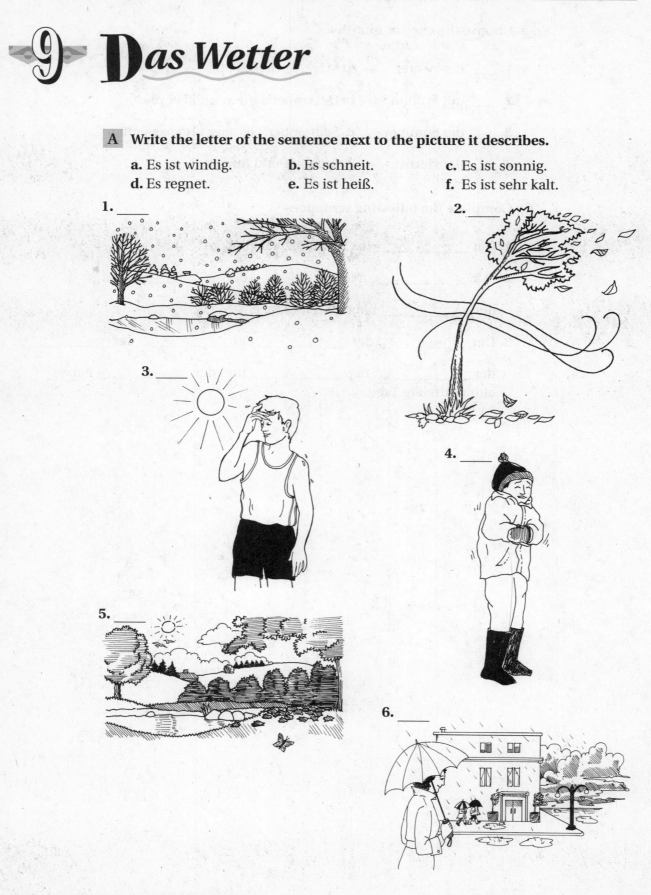

1. ____

2. ____

3. ____

4. ____

5. ____

6. ____

B **Indicate if these statements are *richtig* (R) or *falsch* (F).**

1. ____ Es schneit im Winter.

2. ____ Es ist immer sehr sonnig im April.

3. ____ Es regnet im April.

4. ____ Es ist sehr warm im Dezember.

5. ____ Es ist nicht zu warm. Es ist nicht zu kalt. Es ist kühl.

C **Circle the expressions that describe the topic sentence correctly. There may be more than one correct answer.**

1. Das Wetter ist schön.
   a. Es ist sonnig.
   b. Es ist bewölkt.
   c. Es regnet.
   d. Es ist warm.
   e. Es ist nicht kalt.

2. Es ist schlecht.
   a. Es regnet.
   b. Es ist sonnig.
   c. Das Wetter ist nicht schön.
   d. Es ist sehr kalt.
   e. Es ist schön.

WELCOME TO GERMAN

10 Ich heiße... und ich komme aus...

A Choose the correct question word, *wie* or *woher,* to complete each statement in the picture.

Tag. _____ heißt du?

Und _____ kommst du, Dieter?

Ich heiße Dieter.

Ich komme aus Bremerhaven.

B Choose the correct completion.

1. Wie _____ du?
   a. heiße
   b. heißt

2. Ich _____ Erika.
   a. heiße
   b. heißt

3. Woher _____ du, Erika?
   a. komme
   b. kommst

4. Ich _____ aus Stuttgart.
   a. komme
   b. kommst

5. Woher _____ Sie, Herr Brecht?
   a. kommst
   b. kommen

C Answer the following personal questions.

1. Wie heißt du? _____

2. Woher kommst du? _____

WELCOME TO GERMAN

D **See how much German you know. Match each picture with the correct sentence.**

　　a. Er singt.　　　　**b.** Sie schwimmt.　　　　**c.** Sie lernt.

1. ____

2. ____

3. ____

E **Complete the following.**

1. Sing _____ du? Ja, ich singe.

2. Schwimm _____ du im Sommer? Ja, ich schwimme im Sommer.

3. Studier _____ du viel? Ja, ich studiere viel.

4. Lern _____ du? Ja, ich lern _____.

ⒶReading in German

A Read the following story about Werner and Barbara. You will be amazed how easy it is to read in German.

Werner ist ein Freund von Barbara und Barbara ist eine Freundin von Werner. Werner ist fünfzehn Jahre alt und er kommt aus Deutschland. Er kommt aus München. Natürlich spricht Werner Deutsch. Er spricht auch Englisch, aber er spricht nicht so gut. Er spricht nur ein bißchen Englisch.

Barbara kommt nicht aus Deutschland. Sie kommt aus den USA, aus Amerika. Barbara ist auch fünfzehn Jahre alt. Barbara spricht Englisch und Deutsch. Sie spricht sehr gut Deutsch. Sie spricht immer Deutsch mit Werner.

B It is sometimes necessary to guess at the meaning of a new word when reading. You can very often get the meaning of a new word from the way the word is used in the sentence. This is called getting "meaning from context." From the context of these sentences, guess the meaning of the word *spricht*.

Werner kommt aus Deutschland. Werner spricht Deutsch.
Barbara kommt aus den USA. Barbara spricht Englisch.

Spricht means _____

C Answer the following questions.

1. Wer ist ein Freund von Barbara? _____

2. Wer ist eine Freundin von Werner? _____

3. Wer kommt aus Deutschland? _____

4. Wer kommt aus den USA? _____

5. Wer spricht ein bißchen Englisch? _____

6. Wer spricht Englisch und Deutsch? _____

7. Woher kommt Werner? _____

8. Woher kommt Barbara? _____

Welcome to
Japanese!

Jiko shookai

A Select the correct response. Circle the corresponding letter.

1. What do you say in Japanese to a person you have just been introduced to?
  a. Sumimasen.
  b. Doozo yoroshiku.
  c. Soo desu.

2. What would you say if you wanted to excuse yourself to get someone's attention because you want to speak?
  a. Sumimasen.
  b. Doozo yoroshiku.
  c. Hajimemashite.

3. How would you ask someone if he/she is the person you think he/she is?
  a. Hanada desu.
  b. Hai, soo desu.
  c. Hanada-san desu ka[?]

4. What would you say if you wanted to tell someone who you are?
  a. (name) desu.
  b. (name) -san desu.
  c. Hai, soo desu.

B Select the correct answer.

1. When do you use the title *-san* in Japanese?
  a. When speaking about myself and using my own name.
  b. When using another person's name.

C Choose the correct missing words to complete the following conversation.

a. desu   **b.** ka   **c.** soo   **d.** doozo

—Hanada-san desu ____[?]

—Hai, ____ desu.

—Buraun ____. Hajimemashite. ____ yoroshiku.

2 G*o-aisatsu*

A **Select the appropriate greeting for the time of the day.**

    a. Ohayoo gozaimasu.   **b.** Konnichi wa.   **c.** Konban wa.

1. _____   2. _____

3. _____

B **Indicate whether or not the following mini-conversations make sense.**

	Yes	No
1. —Konnichi wa. —Konnichi wa.	____	____
2. —Ohayoo gozaimasu. —Konban wa.	____	____
3. —O-genki desu ka? —Ee, genki desu.	____	____

C **Circle possible responses to the question:** *O-genki desu ka[?]*

    a. Okagesama de, genki desu.
    b. Konnichi wa.
    c. Genki desu.
    d. Hai, arigatoo gozaimasu.
    e. Sumimasen.

WELCOME TO JAPANESE

D **Select the correct answer and circle the corresponding letter.**

1. Instead of saying *O-genki desu ka[?]* to a person you have seen recently, what would you more commonly say?
   a. Sumimasen.
   b. Ii o-tenki desu ne[?]
   c. Okagesama de, genki desu.

2. How would you respond to the question *Ii o-tenki desu ne[?]*
   a. Genki desu.
   b. Hajimemashite.
   c. Ee, soo desu ne.

E **Select what you would say.**
   a. ne　　　　　　　　**b.** ne(e)

1. _____ You agree with what a person has just said to you.

2. _____ You want to find out if the person you're speaking to agrees with you.

F *Desu* **is a frequently used word in Japanese. Complete the following with *desu*. Then practice these short conversations with a classmate.**

1. —Sumimasen. Hanada-san _____ ka[?]

   —Hai, soo _____.

   —Buraun _____.

2. —Ii o-tenki _____ ne[?]

   —Ee, soo _____ ne.

3. —O-genki _____ ka[?]

   —Hai, arigatoo gozaimasu. Yamaguchi-san wa[?]

   —Genki _____.

3 Wakareru toki ni...

A Indicate if the following expressions are greetings or farewells.

	Greeting	Farewell
1. Ohayoo gozaimasu.	____	____
2. Shitsurei shimasu.	____	____
3. Sayoonara.	____	____
4. Konnichi wa.	____	____
5. Dewa, mata.	____	____

B Select the correct completion to each statement or question. Then practice these short conversations with a classmate.

a. Ohayoo.
b. Soo desu ne.
c. Hai, soo desu.
d. Ee, genki desu.
e. Dewa, mata.

1. —Hanada-san desu ka[?]

_____

2. —Hanada-san, ohayoo gozaimasu.

_____

3. —O-genki desu ka[?]

_____

4. —Ii o-tenki desu ne[?]

_____

5. —Shitsurei shimasu.

_____

WELCOME TO JAPANESE

4 *Kyooshitsu*

A **Match the illustration with the word.**

a. hon
b. kaban
c. chooku
d. keisanki
e. booru-pen
f. nooto
g. enpitsu
h. konpyuutaa

1. ____

2. ____

3. ____

4. ____

5. ____

6. ____

7. ____

8. ____

5 Suu-ji

A Give the correct numeral.

1. ichi _____   7. go-juu-go _____

2. juu-ichi _____   8. hachi _____

3. ni-juu-ichi _____   9. juu-hachi _____

4. go _____   10. hachi-juu _____

5. juu-go _____   11. hachi-juu-hachi _____

6. go-juu _____

B Write the numbers in Japanese using Roman (English) letters.

1. 1 _____   6. 26 _____

2. 5 _____   7. 8 _____

3. 10 _____   8. 88 _____

4. 20 _____   9. 100 _____

5. 50 _____   10. 79 _____

C Add up the numbers on the dominos and write them using Roman (English) letters.

1. _____

2. _____

3. _____

4. _____

5. _____

6. _____

7. _____

8. _____

WELCOME TO JAPANESE

6 Jikan

A Match the correct time with the clock. Write the correct letter in the space provided.

1. ____

2. ____

3. ____

4. ____

5. ____

    a. —Nan-ji desu ka[?]
       —Ni-ji han desu.
    b. —Nan-ji desu ka[?]
       —Roku-ji desu.
    c. —Nan-ji desu ka[?]
       —Juu-ichi-ji han desu.
    d. —Nan-ji desu ka[?]
       —San-ji desu.
    e. —Nan-ji desu ka[?]
       —Ku-ji han desu.

WELCOME TO JAPANESE

7 Resutoran de...

A Match the word with the illustration.

a. supagetti   b. piza   c. sarada
d. juusu   e. hanbaagaa   f. omuretsu

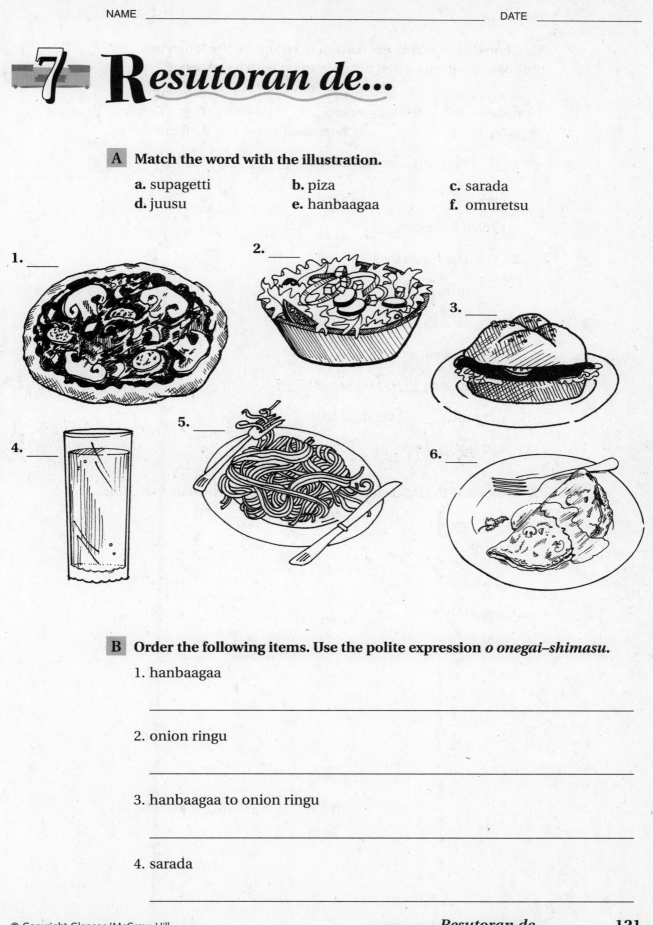

1. _____

2. _____

3. _____

4. _____

5. _____

6. _____

B Order the following items. Use the polite expression *o onegai–shimasu.*

1. hanbaagaa

_____

2. onion ringu

_____

3. hanbaagaa to onion ringu

_____

4. sarada

_____

Resutoran de...   **121**

WELCOME TO JAPANESE

C **Choose the correct expression to complete the following mini-conversations. Then practice them with a classmate.**

a. arimasu   b. to   c. Sumimasen
d. desu   e. hai   f. gozaimasu
g. ka   h. onegai-shimasu   i. ikura

1. ____. Chiizu baagaa wa arimasu ____[?]

   Hai, ____.

   Chiizu baagaa o ____.

2. ____. Hanbaagaa wa ____ ka[?]

   ____, arimasu.

   ____ desu ka[?]

   200-en desu.

3. Hanbaagaa ____ orenji juusu o ____.

   Arigatoo ____. Ikura desu ka[?]

   450-en ____.

D **Indicate if the following Japanese dishes are meat or fish dishes.**

	Meat	Fish
1. sushi	____	____
2. sukiyaki	____	____
3. shabu shabu	____	____
4. tempura	____	____

8 Nani-go o hanashimasu ka[?]

A Select the appropriate word to complete each sentence.

a. Iie   b. Hai   c. sukoshi

1. Hanashimasu ka[?]

_____, hanashimasu.

2. Wakarimasu ka[?]

_____, wakarimasu.

3. Nihongo o hanashimasu ka[?]

_____, _____ hanashimasu.

4. Nihongo o hanashimasu ka[?]

_____, hanashimasen.

B Change the following sentences to the negative.

1. Nihongo o hanashimasu.

_____

2. Eigo ga wakarimasu.

_____

WELCOME TO JAPANESE

⑨ Nan-nichi, nan-yoobi

A Match the days.

1. ____ Sunday   **a.** kin'yoobi

2. ____ Friday   **b.** suiyoobi

3. ____ Monday   **c.** nichiyoobi

4. ____ Wednesday   **d.** getsuyoobi

B Write the numerals for the following numbers.

1. ichi   _____

2. san   _____

3. go   _____

4. shichi   _____

5. ku   _____

6. juu-ichi   _____

C Select which month the following holidays take place in the U.S.

1. ____ Labor Day   **a.** ichi-gatsu

2. ____ Christmas   **b.** juu-ni-gatsu

3. ____ Thanksgiving   **c.** go-gatsu

4. ____ New Year's   **d.** juu-ichi-gatsu

5. ____ Memorial Day   **e.** ku-gatsu

Audio Activities Booklet

WELCOME TO SPANISH

1 Saludos

A Listen and repeat.

B Listen and choose.

    1. a.   b.   c.

    2. a.   b.   c.

    3. a.   b.   c.

C Listen and repeat.

D Listen and choose.

Adiós

A **Listen and repeat.**

B **Listen and choose.**

1. a.   b.   c.

2. a.   b.   c.

3. a.   b.   c.

4. a.   b.   c.

C **Listen and repeat.**

D **Listen and choose.**

1. muchacha   muchacho
2. muchacha   muchacho
3. muchacha   muchacho
4. muchacha   muchacho
5. muchacha   muchacho
6. muchacha   muchacho

3 En clase

A Listen and repeat.

B Listen and choose.

1. _____
2. _____
3. _____
4. _____
5. _____
6. _____

C Listen and ask.

1.
2.
3.
4.
5.

4 Números

A Listen and repeat.

B Listen and choose.

1. _____ 2. _____ 3. _____ 4. _____ 5. _____

C Listen and repeat.

D Listen and choose.

1. _____ 2. _____ 3. _____ 4. _____ 5. _____

E Listen and repeat.

F Listen and repeat.

G Listen and answer.

5 La cortesía

A Listen and repeat.

B Listen and ask.

1.

2.

3.

4.

C Listen and answer.

40 pesos

30 pesos

100 pesos

70 pesos

6 La hora

WELCOME TO SPANISH

A Listen and repeat.

B Listen and repeat.

C Listen and answer.

1. _____

2. _____

3. _____

4. _____

5. _____

6. _____

D Listen and answer.

1. _____

2. _____

3. _____

4. _____

CURSOS	HORA
Matemáticas	8:00
Español	10:30
Inglés	2:00
Ciencias	1:15

WELCOME TO SPANISH

7 Los colores

A Listen and repeat.

B Listen and answer.

1. _____
2. _____
3. _____
4. _____

8 Los días de la semana

A Listen and repeat.

B Listen and answer.

1. _____ 2. _____
3. _____ 4. _____
5. _____ 6. _____

C Listen and choose.

1. ____ 2. ____ 3. ____ 4. ____

5. ____ 6. ____ 7. ____

⑨ Los meses y las estaciones

A Listen and repeat.

B Listen and choose.

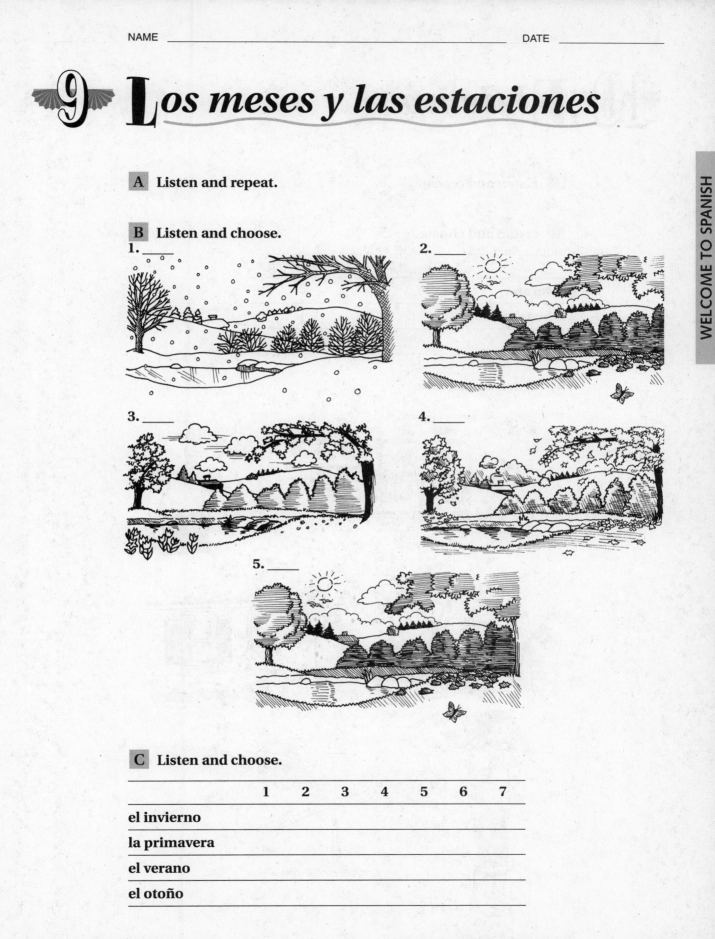

1. _____

2. _____

3. _____

4. _____

5. _____

C Listen and choose.

	1	2	3	4	5	6	7
el invierno							
la primavera							
el verano							
el otoño							

10 El tiempo

A Listen and repeat.

B Listen and choose.

	1	2	3	4	5
el verano					
el invierno					
los dos					

C Listen and choose.

WELCOME TO SPANISH

11 Yo soy...

A Listen and repeat.

B Listen and choose.

	1	2	3	4	5	6
verdad						
falso						

12 Soy de...

A Listen and repeat.

B Listen and repeat.

C Listen and choose.

1. Sí   No   **2.** Sí   No

3. Sí   No   **4.** Sí   No

5. Sí   No   **6.** Sí   No

D Listen and choose.

1. a.   b.   c.

2. a.   b.   c.

3. a.   b.   c.

Audio Activities Booklet   **135**

13 Hablo español

A   Listen and repeat.

B   Listen and react.

1. _____   2. _____

3. _____   4. _____

5. _____   6. _____

7. _____   8. _____

14 Estudio...

A   Listen and repeat.

B   Listen and choose.

1. a.   b.   c.   2. a.   b.   c.

3. a.   b.   c.

C   Listen and answer.

$X = X^2 + 5XY + Y^2$

15 M*i casa*

A Listen and repeat.

B Listen and choose.

1. a.   b.   c.

2. a.   b.   c.

3. a.   b.   c.

4. a.   b.   c.

C Listen and answer.

16 M*i familia*

A Listen and repeat.

B Listen and answer.

Isabel   Antonio

Carlos   Antonia   María   Armando

Lupita   Juan   Pedro   Yo   Ana

	1	2	3	4	5	6	7	8
verdad								
falso								

C Listen and repeat.

17 M*i mascota*

A **Listen and repeat.**

B **Listen and repeat.**

C **Listen and choose.**

D **Listen and choose.**

1. a.   b.   c.   2. a.   b.   c.

3. a.   b.   c.   4. a.   b.   c.

5. a.   b.   c.   6. a.   b.   c.

18 L*os deportes*

A Listen and repeat.

B Listen and choose.

C Listen and choose.

1. a.   b.

2. a.   b.

3. a.   b.

4. a.   b.

5. a.   b.

19 La ropa

A Listen and repeat.

B Listen and choose.

Audio Activities Booklet **141**

1 **L***es salutations*

A Listen and repeat.

B Listen and choose.

	1	2	3	4
vrai				
faux				

C Listen and repeat.

D Listen and choose.

❖2❖ **A**u revoir

A **Listen and repeat.**

B **Listen and choose.**

	1	2	3	4	5
vrai					
faux					

C **Listen and repeat.**

D **Listen and choose.**

1. jeune fille   garçon
2. jeune fille   garçon
3. jeune fille   garçon
4. jeune fille   garçon
5. jeune fille   garçon
6. jeune fille   garçon

❸ **E**n classe

A Listen and repeat.

B Listen and choose.

1. un cahier ____
2. un stylo-bille ____
3. une gomme ____
4. un bloc ____
5. un livre ____
6. un crayon ____

C Listen and ask.

4 *L**es nombres*

A Listen and repeat.

B Listen and add.

1. _____   2. _____

3. _____   4. _____

5. _____

C Listen and repeat.

D Listen and circle.

1.	20	15	50		6.	38	67	61
2.	25	5	17		7.	100	11	1
3.	53	10	70		8.	25	31	7
4.	70	34	15		9.	46	29	6
5.	92	26	9		10.	20	98	40

E Listen and repeat.

F Listen and repeat.

G Listen and answer.

5 La politesse

A Listen and repeat.

B Listen and choose.

	1	2	3	4
vrai				
faux				

6 L'heure

A Listen and repeat.

B Listen and repeat.

C Listen and choose.

7 ❖ Les couleurs

A Listen and repeat.

B Listen and answer.

1. _____

2. _____

3. _____

4. _____

8 ❖ Les jours de la semaine

A Listen and repeat.

B Listen and answer.

1. _____ 2. _____

3. _____ 4. _____

5. _____ 6. _____

7. _____ 8. _____

C Listen and decide.

____ lundi   ____ mardi   ____ mercredi

____ jeudi   ____ vendredi   ____ samedi

____ dimanche

9 Les mois et les saisons

A Listen and repeat.

B Listen and choose.

	1	2	3	4	5	6	7
printemps							
été							
automne							
hiver							

C Listen and answer.

1. _____

2. _____

3. _____

4. _____

5. _____

6. _____

10 Le temps

A Listen and repeat.

B Listen and choose.

	1	2	3	4	5
en été					
en hiver					
les deux					

C Listen and choose.

WELCOME TO FRENCH

Je suis...

A Listen and repeat.

B Listen and choose.

	1	2	3	4	5
vrai					
faux					

 Je suis de...

A Listen and repeat.

B Listen and repeat.

C Listen and choose.

1. Oui.   Non.   2. Oui.   Non.

3. Oui.   Non.   4. Oui.   Non.

5. Oui.   Non.   6. Oui.   Non.

D Listen and choose.

	1	2	3	4	5	6
vrai						
faux						

WELCOME TO FRENCH

13 Je parle français

A Listen and repeat.

B Listen and react.

1. _____

2. _____

3. _____

4. _____

5. _____

6. _____

7. _____

8. _____

Audio Activities Booklet   **151**

WELCOME TO FRENCH

14 J'aime...

A Listen and repeat.

B Listen and answer.

1. _____
2. _____
3. _____
4. _____
5. _____

C Listen and answer.

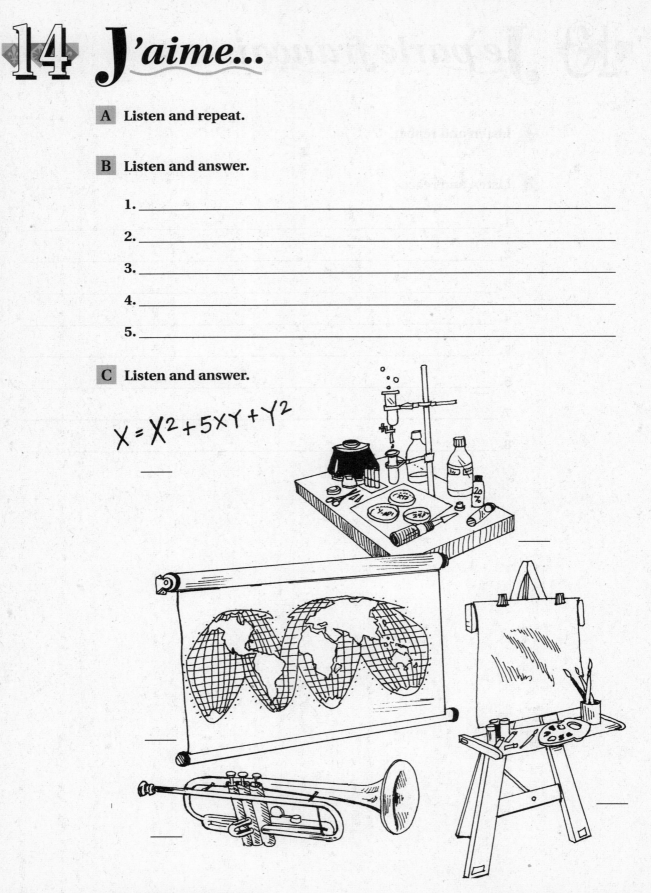

$$X = X^2 + 5XY + Y^2$$

15 Ma maison

A **Listen and repeat.**

B **Listen and choose.**

1. a.   b.   c.

2. a.   b.   c.

3. a.   b.   c.

4. a.   b.   c.

C **Listen and answer.**

Audio Activities Booklet **153**

16 Ma famille

A Listen and repeat.

B Listen and choose.

	1	2	3	4	5	6	7	8
vrai								
faux								

C Listen and repeat.

D Listen and repeat.

17 Un bon ami

A Listen and repeat.

B Listen and repeat.

C Listen and choose.

____   ____   ____

____   ____   ____

____   ____

D Listen and answer.

1. _____

2. _____

3. _____

4. _____

5. _____

6. _____

18 Les sports

A Listen and repeat.

B Listen and choose.

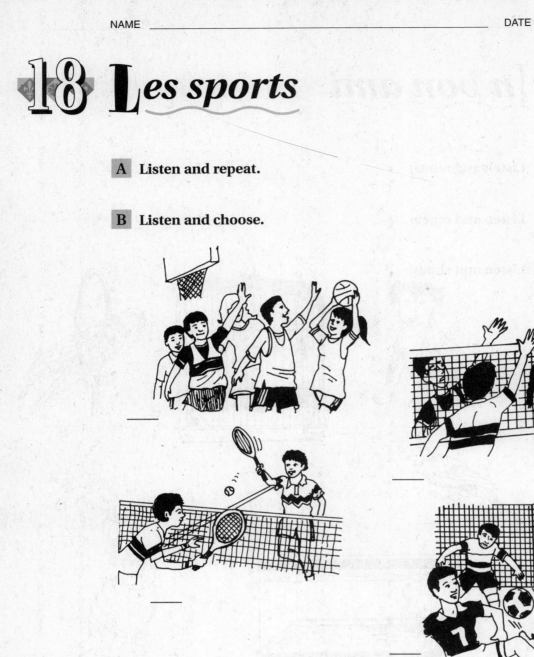

_____

_____

_____

_____

C Listen and choose.

	1	2	3	4	5
soccer					
tennis					
both					
neither					

Invitation to Languages

19 Les vêtements

A Listen and repeat.

B Listen and choose.

Audio Activities Booklet **157**

1 Ciao!

A Listen and repeat.

B Listen and choose.

Ciao.	_____	Buona sera.	_____
Come sta?	_____	Non c'è male.	_____
Buon giorno.	_____	Bene.	_____
Come stai?	_____	Grazie.	_____

C Listen and repeat.

D Listen and choose.

	1	2	3	4	5
vero					
falso					

2 Arrivederci!

A Listen and repeat.

B Listen and choose.

1. a.   b.   c.   2. a.   b.   c.

3. a.   b.   c.   4. a.   b.   c.

C Listen and repeat.

D Listen and choose.

In classe

A Listen and repeat.

B Listen and choose.

1. _____
2. _____
3. _____
4. _____
5. _____
6. _____

C Listen and choose.

WELCOME TO ITALIAN

Numeri

A Listen and repeat.

B Listen and repeat.

C Listen and repeat.

D Listen and write.

1. ____ 2. ____ 3. ____ 4. ____ 5. ____

6. ____ 7. ____ 8. ____ 9. ____ 10. ____

E Listen and repeat.

F Listen and answer.

Audio Activities Booklet   **161**

5 Prego

A Listen and repeat.

B Listen and choose.

	1	2	3	4	5	6
vero						
falso						

C Listen and answer.

4€   3€   1€

6 *Che ora è?*

A Listen and repeat.

B Listen and repeat.

C Listen and choose.

(P.M.)

D Listen and choose.

	1	2	3	4	5	6	7
vero							
falso							

WELCOME TO ITALIAN

7 I *giorni della settimana*

A Listen and repeat.

B Listen and answer.

1. _____

2. _____

3. _____

4. _____

5. _____

6. _____

7. _____

C Listen and choose.

1.   **Sì.**   **No.**

2.   **Sì.**   **No.**

3.   **Sì.**   **No.**

4.   **Sì.**   **No.**

5.   **Sì.**   **No.**

8 Mesi e stagioni

A Listen and repeat.

B Listen and repeat.

C Listen and choose.

primavera	_____	giugno	_____
luglio	_____	estate	_____
marzo	_____	autunno	_____
dicembre	_____	febbraio	_____
aprile	_____	maggio	_____

9 Il tempo

A Listen and repeat.

B Listen and choose.

1. a.   b.   c.   2. a.   b.   c.

3. a.   b.   c.   4. a.   b.   c.

5. a.   b.   c.

Audio Activities Booklet   **165**

WELCOME TO ITALIAN

10 Sono...

A Listen and repeat.

B Listen and repeat.

C Listen and choose.

	1	2	3	4	5
vero					
falso					

11 Parlo italiano

A Listen and repeat.

B Listen and answer.

1. _____

2. _____

3. _____

4. _____

C Listen and choose.

	1	2	3	4	5	6
vero						
falso						

1 Salvē et Valē

A Listen and repeat.

B Listen and choose.

1. a.   b.   c.

2. a.   b.   c.

3. a.   b.   c.

2 Numerī

A Listen and repeat.

B Listen and choose.

1. ____   2. ____   3. ____   4. ____   5. ____

C Listen and add.

1. _____   2. _____

3. _____   4. _____

5. _____   6. _____

D Listen and subtract.

1. _____   2. _____

3. _____   4. _____

5. _____

WELCOME TO LATIN

3 Paulus et Clāra

A Listen and repeat.

B Listen and choose.

1. _____   2. _____   3. _____   4. _____

C Listen and react.

1. _____   2. _____
3. _____   4. _____
5. _____

4 Amīcī et Discipulī

A Listen and repeat.

B Listen and react.

1. _____   2. _____
3. _____   4. _____
5. _____

C Listen and decide.

1. _____   2. _____
3. _____   4. _____
5. _____   6. _____

WELCOME TO LATIN

5 Amīcus amīcam videt

A Listen and repeat.

B Listen and decide.

1. _____   2. _____

3. _____   4. _____

5. _____

C Listen and decide.

1. _____   2. _____

3. _____   4. _____

5. _____

1 Begrüßung

A Listen and repeat.

B Listen and choose.

	1	2	3	4
richtig				
falsch				

C Listen and repeat.

D Listen and choose.

	1	2	3	4	5	6
formal						
informal						

2 Verabschieden

A Listen and repeat.

B Listen and repeat.

C Listen and choose.

	1	2	3	4	5	6
richtig						
falsch						

D Listen and choose.

	1	2	3	4	5
richtig					
falsch					

WELCOME TO GERMAN

3 Im Klassenzimmer

A Listen and repeat.

B Listen and choose.

1. a.　　　　b.　　　　c.

2. a.　　　　b.　　　　c.

3. a.　　　　b.　　　　c.

C Listen and choose.

____ **1.** der Kugelschreiber   ____ **2.** der Bleistift

____ **3.** der Schwamm   ____ **4.** der Block

____ **5.** das Buch   ____ **6.** das Papier

____ **7.** ein Stück Papier   ____ **8.** der Computer

____ **9.** der Rechner   ____ **10.** der Stuhl

____ **11.** der Schreibtisch   ____ **12.** der Rucksack

4 **D***ie* **Zahlen**

A Listen and repeat.

B Listen and choose.

1. _____ 2. _____

3. _____ 4. _____

5. _____ 6. _____

C Listen and repeat.

D Listen and choose.

1. _____ 2. _____

3. _____ 4. _____

5. _____

E Listen and repeat.

F Listen and choose.

	1	2	3	4
richtig				
falsch				

WELCOME TO GERMAN

#

A Listen and repeat.

B Listen and ask.

1.

2.

3.

4.

C Listen and choose.

1. a.   b.   c.

2. a.   b.   c.

3. a.   b.   c.

⑥ **D**ie Uhrzeit

A Listen and repeat.

B Listen and repeat.

C Listen and choose.

1.

2.

3.

4.

5.

6.

D Listen and choose.

	1	2	3	4	5
richtig					
falsch					

WELCOME TO GERMAN

7 **D**ie *Tage*

A Listen and repeat.

B Listen and answer.

1. _____

2. _____

3. _____

4. _____

5. _____

6. _____

C Listen and choose.

1. a.   b.   c.

2. a.   b.   c.

3. a.   b.   c.

WELCOME TO GERMAN

Die Monate und die Jahreszeiten

A Listen and repeat.

B Listen and choose.

	1	2	3	4	5
richtig					
falsch					

C Listen and choose.

1. a.   b.   c.

2. a.   b.   c.

3. a.   b.   c.

4. a.   b.   c.

WELCOME TO GERMAN

9 **D***as Wetter*

A **Listen and repeat.**

B **Listen and choose.**

	1	2	3	4	5
im Sommer					
im Winter					

C **Listen and identify.**

10 *Ich heiße... und ich komme aus...*

A Listen and repeat.

B Listen and choose.

1. Ja. Nein.

2. Ja. Nein.

3. Ja. Nein.

4. Ja. Nein.

5. Ja. Nein.

6. Ja. Nein.

C Listen and choose.

	1	2	3	4	5	6
richtig						
falsch						

WELCOME TO GERMAN

Jiko shookai

A Listen and repeat.

B Listen.

C Listen and choose.

    1. a.   b.   c.   2. a.   b.   c.

2 Go-aisatsu

A Listen and repeat.

B Listen and repeat.

C Listen.

D Listen and choose.

	1	2	3	4	5
true					
false					

E Listen and match.

a.   b.   c.

1. a.   b.   c.

2. a.   b.   c.

3. a.   b.   c.

WELCOME TO JAPANESE

3 Wakareru toki ni...

A Listen and repeat.

B Listen.

C Listen and choose.

	1	2	3	4	5
true					
false					

D Listen and react.

1. _____

2. _____

3. _____

4. _____

5. _____

Kyooshitsu

A Listen and repeat.

B Listen.

C Listen and choose.

	1	2	3	4	5
true					
false					

5 **S**uu-ji

A Listen and repeat.

B Listen and choose.

1. _____   2. _____

3. _____   4. _____

5. _____

C Listen and repeat.

D Listen and choose.

1. _____   2. _____

3. _____   4. _____

5. _____

Audio Activities Booklet   **183**

WELCOME TO JAPANESE

6 Jikan

A Listen and repeat.

B Listen and choose.

C Listen.

D Listen and choose.

1. a.   b.   c.   2. a.   b.   c.

7 Resutoran de...

A Listen and repeat.

B Listen and choose.

	1	2	3	4	5
hungry					
thirsty					

C Listen and repeat.

D Listen and choose.

1. a.   b.   c.

2. a.   b.   c.

3. a.   b.   c.

E Listen and choose.

	1	2	3	4	5	6	7	8	9	10
Nihon ryoori										
Amerika ryoori										

WELCOME TO JAPANESE

Nani-go o hanashimasu ka[?]

A Listen and repeat.

B Listen and react.

1. _____

2. _____

3. _____

4. _____

5. _____

6. _____

7. _____

WELCOME TO JAPANESE

9 Nan-yichi, nan-yoobi

A Listen and repeat.

B Listen and answer.

1. _____

2. _____

3. _____

4. _____

5. _____

6. _____

7. _____

C Listen and repeat.

D Listen and match.

Yoko   hachi-gatsu

Noriko   ichi-gatsu

Michiko   ni-gatsu

Kiyoshi   go-gatsu

Haruko   juu-ni-gatsu

Kasumi   shi-gatsu

                             juu-ichi-gatsu

                             shichi-gatsu

                             san-gatsu

                             roko-gatsu

WELCOME TO JAPANESE